The Golden Book of
LOST WORLDS

GREAT CIVILIZATIONS OF THE PAST

Over 4,000 years old, this little bronze stag is one of many found in the tombs of the ancient kings of Alaja Huyuk, near the modern city of Ankara, Turkey.

The Golden Book of

LOST WORLDS

Great Civilizations of the Past

ADAPTED FOR YOUNG READERS
BY JANET CHENERY

FROM *The Horizon Book of Lost Worlds*
BY THE EDITORS OF *Horizon Magazine*

EDITOR IN CHARGE MARSHALL B. DAVIDSON
NARRATIVE BY LEONARD COTTRELL

GOLDEN PRESS NEW YORK

FRONTISPIECE

Four sculptured heads recall the ancient nations that have since disappeared from the earth. At left is the bronze head of an Elamite priest or ruler from south-western Iran; next is Gudea, the powerful ruler of Lagash; the third is a god of the ancient Etruscans, called the Apollo of Veii; the fourth, at right, is a stone portrait of the Egyptian Queen Hatshepsut who ruled as pharaoh during part of the period called the New Kingdom, nearly 1500 years before the Christian era.

LIBRARY OF CONGRESS CATALOG CARD NUMBER: 63-14920

ENGLISH-LANGUAGE EDITION © 1962, 1963 BY AMERICAN HERITAGE PUBLISHING CO. INC.
ALL RIGHTS RESERVED UNDER BERNE AND PAN-AMERICAN COPYRIGHT CONVENTIONS.
REPRODUCTION IN WHOLE OR IN PART WITHOUT PERMISSION IS PROHIBITED.
DESIGNED AND PRODUCED BY ARTISTS AND WRITERS PRESS, INC.
PRINTED IN THE U.S.A. BY WESTERN PRINTING AND LITHOGRAPHING COMPANY.
PUBLISHED BY GOLDEN PRESS, INC., NEW YORK. PUBLISHED SIMULTANEOUSLY
IN CANADA BY THE MUSSON BOOK COMPANY, LTD., TORONTO.

contents

*Although the exact origin of this little statuette is
unknown, its feet, with their large curling toes, are
typically Hittite and the ibex horn on its head is a
common motif among peoples of the Asian steppes.*

This famous bust portrait of Queen Nefretiti is the finest work of art left to us from Egypt's Amarna period.

preface

BETWEEN 8000 and 7000 B.C., wandering tribesmen who lived near the Arabian, Syrian and Iranian deserts began to leave their caves and temporary shelters and gathered together in more or less fixed communities. Instead of constantly roaming in search of wild fruits and grain, they learned to plant seeds and to cultivate crops. Instead of hunting wild animals, they learned to domesticate and breed goats and pigs, thereby freeing themselves from the unending struggle for food and shelter.

Life now became more abundant and secure than ever before. By about 4000 B.C. some communities had so increased their production of food that they were not only able to support their growing populations, but also to use much of their time and energies for other activities. Within the three or four thousand years since they ceased their nomadic existence, the conditions of life had changed more radically than they had over the entire preceding quarter of a million years.

Yet the next thousand years witnessed an even more spectacular revolution. With the elementary problems of agriculture and stock breeding solved, men were able to devote themselves to countless experiments and enterprises. This period between about 4000 and 3000 B.C. produced more inventions and discoveries than any other time in human history before the sixteenth century A.D. During these years the basic mechanical principles upon which all the devices of civilization would depend, were first mastered. Weaving, metallurgy, the plow, and the wheel were invented. The technique of molding bricks was discovered,

7

draft animals were harnessed for new sources of motive power, sails were devised to capture the force of the winds, and seals were created and used to distinguish and protect private property.

The first gathering together of human experience, skill, and effort attended both the birth of civilization and the rise of the cities where it first took shape. Although increased wealth and more advanced technology were essential, life at a civilized level also called for new relationships between human beings— economic organization, political controls, and social attitudes, the latter not only among men and their neighbors, but also between them and their gods.

Above all, the rise of civilization depended upon a meeting of minds, and it was in the cities with their market places and temples, their palaces and side streets, that such meetings more readily took place. The very word *civilization* means the making of cities and urban life. And it was in the cities, in the earliest of men's civilizations, that the art of writing was created. This accomplishment was the clearest mark of civilized man for through it, as never before, he could share his experiences, record his old traditions, project his thoughts over distances, and bequeath them to the future.

Nine early civilizations are described in this book. In each, a human society was able to master the inventions and develop the institutions which led to high civilization. In some cases, the record is rich and detailed, while in others it remains a broad outline to be filled in by work in progress and by discoveries yet to be made. While the enormous debt of the Western world to the cultures of ancient Greece and Rome has been almost continually well-known, our and their great debt to even more ancient peoples has only recently become clear. For although each of these ancient worlds developed distinct and complex patterns, and each endured for many centuries, they all faded and withered away, and their remarkable achievements were practically forgotten for ages to come.

Vague memories of these "lost worlds" lingered throughout the centuries in the form of legends from an improbable and remote past. Some nations left imperishable monuments while others vanished under mounds of dust, desert sands, or silt, or were covered by the overwhelming growth of tropical jungles.

Within the past century and a half, however, the science of archaeology has been born, and with it have come astonishing revelations. Combined with the research of scholars and the work of scientists in the laboratory, archaeologists have been able to recover many of the forgotten segments of human history. Much that was long believed to be myth or poetic allegory has been substantiated. The great Tower of Babel, the labyrinthine palace of King Minos, the fabulous Hanging Gardens of Babylon, and other wonders and curiosities of the ancient world have become historical realities.

The worlds of the mighty Sargon and Hammurabi the law-giver, of Assurnasirpal, "the great king, king of Assyria," of Abraham and Moses, of Agamemnon, Priam, and of the mighty Egyptian pharaohs Tuthmosis III and Ramesses II have come alive again before our eyes. So also, the long forgotten civilizations of the Indus River Valley in Pakistan and northern India, the Cambodian jungle realm of the Khmers and the American Maya have been rediscovered.

Although there are still many gaps in our knowledge of these ancient worlds, we can now trace our Western traditions back to the earliest of all civilizations in Mesopotamia—in the land of the Sumer—and in Egypt. The dark-skinned, dark-haired people who came down from the mountains of Iran to settle the marshy lands of the Tigris-Euphrates Valley were the first people in history to develop the arts and practices that constitute civilized life. During the fourth millennium B.C. they had raised great cities with huge temples, devised a system of irrigation, invented a form of writing and created a literature, and learned to use copper and cast bronze for tools and weapons.

Almost simultaneously with the rise of Sumer, another civilization rose on the banks of the Nile. Although Egypt may have owed some debt to the Sumerian culture, it found its principal strength in native forces of mind and spirit—and without the friction and ferment of urban life.

In these two instances, perhaps the only ones in history, the transition from a primitive level of existence to that of a highly civilized life was achieved independently and spontaneously. Although man also created new worlds in the Far East and in Middle America, their origins, for the moment at least, are obscure. Thus, we consider Egypt and Sumer to be the birthplaces of civilization.

For the rest, civilization has been acquired by primitive people from their more advanced fellow men, by peaceful inheritance or violent appropriation, and it has spread along the routes of migration, invasion, and trade.

The ancient Near East, lying across the international highways that link the continents of Africa, Asia and Europe, has played the most important role in the spreading of cultures. The Arabian desert was, so far as we know, the home of the tribes that made up the Semitic peoples. On the steppes to the far north were other tribes whose language was Indo-European. In one of the great continuing movements of history, for millennium after millennium, nomadic people poured out of these two great, relatively barren regions and descended upon the civilized areas of the Near East and the Mediterranean world.

The first Indo-Europeans to appear were the Hittites, from the uplands of central Asia, who asserted their rule over a large part of Asia Minor shortly after 2000 B.C. At the same time another stream of Indo-Europeans spread into Greece, imposing their Greek language upon the earlier inhabitants of the peninsula.

This ornament from the top of a cosmetic box was discovered in Mari, an ancient city on the trading route between Mesopotamia and the Mediterranean.

In the centuries that followed, warrior tribes and torrential hordes of wandering peoples poured into Asia Minor and the Aegean world, and down the Syrian and Palestine coast. Nations rose and fell, powerful dynasties held vast populations in slavery or in benevolent subjugation. By the end of the third century B.C., as Mesopotamia and Egypt drifted into obscurity, a new world was forming beyond the western sea in the jungles of Middle America. And centuries later, as the Maya reached the summit of their achievement and started their decline, the Khmers on the other side of the world were building their great capitol of Angkor Thom in the jungles of Cambodia.

The term civilization implies an advance from a state of barbarism but there is no certain way of measuring one against any other. It would be rash indeed to claim that our contemporary art shows any significant advance over the finest work of the ancient Egyptians or the Khmers, or that we have today achieved a greater harmony of individual and society and nature than did the Minoans of Crete. However, in sharing the adventures of the peoples who developed these forgotten worlds of the past, we may hope to reach a better understanding of what civilization really means. And as we learn about these remote societies, we can only enrich our own experience.

chronology

EGYPT		MESOPOTAMIA		CRETE AND MAINL...
Predynastic Period				
Old Kingdom	**3100–2160**	**Jemdet Nasr Period**	**3200–3000**	
Union of Egypt	3100	Rise of Sumerian city-states	before 3000	
		Early Dynastic Period	**3000–2370**	**Rise of Cretan Civilization**
Third Dynasty	2670–2600			Neolithic settlement at Dimini
Step Pyramid	2650			
Cheops' Pyramid	2575	Royal Tombs at Ur	2500	
		Sargon	c. 2370	
Period of Anarchy	2160–2133	**Sumerian Revival**	**2230–2000**	
		Building of great Ur ziggurat	2100	
Middle Kingdom	**2133–1625**	**Old Babylonian Period**	**2000–1595**	**Mycenaeans Enter Greece**
		Age of Mari	c. 1800	
		Hammurabi	1792–1750	**Height of Cretan Culture**
Rise of Osiris cult				Building of great palaces
				Minoan domination of the sea
				Development of Linear A script
Hyksos Domination	1700–1567			Grave circles at Mycenae
New Kingdom	**1567–1085**	Hittites sack Babylon	1595	
Eighteenth Dynasty	1567–1320	**Middle Babylonian Period**	**after 1595**	
				Development of Linear B script
Empire of Tuthmosis III	1482–1450			**Mycenaeans Rule in Crete**
		Kassites rule Babylon		Destruction of palaces
				and fall of Minoan civilization
Akhenaten	1379–1361			Mycenaean maritime supremacy
Tutankhamen	1361–1352			
Ramesses II	1304–1237			
Temples of Karnak				
and Abu Simbel				Trojan War
Exodus of the Hebrews	1240			Fall of Mycenaean centers
Great Invasion of Sea Peoples	1191			
		Assyrian Period	**1115–612**	**Dorian Invasion**
Late Period	**1085–525**	Conquests of		Final destruction of Mycenae
		Tiglath-pileser I	1115–1077	
				Dark Age
Assyrians conquer Egypt	671	Height of Assyrian power	875–630	
Saite Period	664–525	Fall of Nineveh	612	Homer
		Neo-Babylonian Period	**612–538**	
		Nebuchadnezzar II	c. 600	**Classical Age of Greece**
Persian Domination	**525–404**	**Persian Rule**	**538–331**	Persians invade Greece
Herodotus visits Egypt	c. 450	Herodotus visits Babylon	c. 450	Herodotus
Alexander the Great		Alexander conquers Babylon	331	Alexander the Great
conquers Egypt	332			
Ptolemaic Period	**323–30**			
Cleopatra	69–30			

ECE	ANATOLIA AND THE LEVANT		OTHERS	
3000–1900					30
2700	Egypt trades with Byblos	2600		
	Troy II	2500–2250	**Indus Valley Civilization**	**2500–1500**
	Alaja Huyuk	2400–2200		
					20
2000–1700	**Hittites Enter Anatolia**	**c. 1900**		
after 1700	Assyrian traders at Kultepe	1900		
c. 1750				
1600–1500				
	Mursilis I	1620–1590		
after 1500	**Rise of Mitanni**	**c. 1500**		
after 1500	Phoenicians develop alphabet	c. 1500		
	Hittite Empire	**1460–1200**		
1400?				
1400–1200	Suppululiumas I	1380–1340		
	Battle of Kadesh	1300		
	Collapse of Hittites	1200		
1200	**Phrygian Occupation of Anatolia**	**1200–700**		
c. 1200	Invasions of Sea Peoples	c. 1200		
	Hebrews invade Canaan	c. 1200		
c. 1150				
1100	Neo-Hittite kingdoms in northern Syria	after 1100			10
	Rise of Sidon and Tyre	**c. 1000**	**Villanovan Culture in Italy**	**1000**
	Assyrians Dominate Levant	**875–630**	**Height of Etruscan Civilization**	**800–500**
775?	Phoenicians found Carthage	814?	Founding of Rome	753
492–479	**Persian Conquest of Anatolia and Levant**	**540–538**	Rome expels Tarquins	510
c. 450			**Decline of Etruscans**	**400–200**
c. 330			Gauls invade Italy	400–300
			Rome conquers Veii	396
			Maya Classic Age	**300–900**
			Height of Khmer Civilization	**802–1215**

EGYPT

1: kingdom of the pharaohs

THERE is no landscape in the world quite like that of Egypt. Here, across a thousand miles of desert, rolls the Nile River, bordered on either side by a strip of rich green vegetation. The fertile land beside the river varies in width from a few hundred yards to several miles, and it is this narrow valley band that supports a nation of some twenty million people. Egypt, as Herodotus remarked 2500 years ago, is truly the gift of the Nile.

The colossal stone head of Ramesses II, pharaoh of the thirteenth century B.C., lies broken on the desert sands, a mute reminder of the vanished glory of Egypt.

Far to the south, there are two Niles, the White and the Blue. The White, the main stream, rises in the great lakes of Albert and Victoria in equatorial Africa. The Blue Nile flows down from the high Abyssinian plateau. The two rivers meet south of Khartum and here, annually, the White Nile renews itself. As the Blue Nile and its tributary, the Atbara, become swollen with spring rains and melting snows, they flow down from the mountains carrying a heavy burden of fertile silt, and for awhile they hold back the waters of the White Nile. Then, as the flood subsides, the White Nile is released and speeds across the dry desert.

CYPRUS

LEBANON • Kadesh

Byblos •

SYRIA

Sidon •

• Damascus

MEDITERRANEAN

SEA

Megiddo •

ISRAEL • Jerusalem

JORDAN

Alexandria •   • Buto

Sais •   • Busiris

• Tanis

LOWER
EGYPT

Cairo •

Giza •   • Memphis

Saqqara •

SINAI

Gerza •

FAYUM

el Amarna •

NILE

Deir Tasa •

Badari •

UPPER
EGYPT

Thinis •

Abydos •   • Dendera

VALLEY OF
THE KINGS → Thebes •   • Karnak

Luxor •

Hierakonpolis •

RED

SEA

WADI HAMMAMAT

Edfu •

First Cataract • Aswan

N

Abu Simbel •

Second Cataract

Scale

0   25   50   75 Miles

NUBIA

The important centers of Egypt were never far from their life-line, the Nile River. The pyramids are near Giza, where the river valley begins to fan out into the Delta of Lower Egypt; nearby Memphis was the first capital of the country. Several hundred miles down the Nile is Thebes, the capital of the New Kingdom pharaohs, and close by were Karnak and Luxor, and the magnificent Valley of the Kings, sites of temples and colossi which still attest to the ancient power and splendor of this lost civilization.

Thus also, soil scoured from the highlands of Abyssinia, borne on the summer torrents of the Blue Nile and the Atbara, provides the land with its miraculous fertility which has endowed Egypt with its unique heritage.

Egypt falls naturally into two separate areas, Upper (southern) and Lower (northern); the two areas are divided at the point where the narrow Nile Valley broadens out into the Delta. Upper Egypt comprises the long river valley from the great rapids called the First Cataract, near Aswan, down to Cairo. Lower Egypt spreads like a huge fan from Cairo northward to the Mediterranean Sea.

In contrast to the vast desert sands and the fertile valley are cliffs of golden limestone, from which the Egyptians quarried their building blocks and tunneled their tombs. But most imposing in this alien land are the pyramids, man-made mountains reaching into the sky, and the soaring stone columns of ancient temples, bigger than forest trees and crowned with huge capitals that are hewn in the shapes of papyrus and lotus buds.

The origins of Egyptian civilization have been found in the deserts that flank the valley. There, in the limestone cliffs and nearby valleys, paleontologists have discovered stone implements and cave shelters containing the bones of animals such as the hippopotamus and buffalo, gazelle and wild ass. The earliest ancestors of the ancient Egyptians were hunters who pursued these animals over 12,000 years ago, when prairies existed over the lands where today's deserts lie.

Between 5000 and 4000 B.C., men began to move down into the Nile Valley. At that time hundreds of kinds of animals still lived near the river; crocodiles and hippopotamuses basked with their snouts just above the muddy water; wildfowl rose in clouds from the papyrus reeds where the hunters poled their light skiffs; game was plentiful, and harpoons and throwing sticks flashed in the sunlight, and nets were lowered from the frail boats, to be drawn up again heavily laden with fishes. This great abundance continued well into historic times and, in later centuries, was recorded in the tomb paintings and reliefs that pictured life along the river.

The pharaoh Mycerinus stands alongside his queen in an idealized stone portrait, typical of the rigidly conventional sculptures of the Old Kingdom artists.

The primitive Egyptian studied the animals around him in order to hunt them for food, and also to protect himself against them. But he also worshiped them, because they possessed powers that were superior to his own. In time, certain animals became associated with human characteristics that they seemed to symbolize. The swift, fierce falcon became one of the insignia of royalty; the crocodile, lion, and hippopotamus were combined in an infernal monster that devoured guilty souls; the lion, given a regal human head, became the sphinx, symbolizing kingly majesty; and the tall, storklike ibis with its thoughtful appearance became Thoth, the god of wisdom and of writing.

During the fifth millennium B.C. and into the early part of the fourth, the early Egyptian hunters began to become farmers, too. They grew wheat and barley and stored the grain in mat-lined pits. Using bone needles, they made clothes of animal skins, and they wore bracelets of shell and ivory, beads of pierced stone, ivory and bone combs. They also ground up malachite to make green eye paint, on slate palettes which were often carved in the shape of animals or birds. They continued to use flint for their tools and weapons, though copper objects were beginning to be made, too. They fashioned earthernware vessels of excellent workmanship, and made vases hollowed out of stone from the cliffs along the Nile.

This era is referred to as the Predynastic Period; (later Egyptian history is recorded in periods called dynasties, each dynasty representing the several generations of any one family which ruled the land).

The Predynastic Period came to a startling conclusion around the end of the fourth millennium. Then, in an extraordinarily short period of about 300 years, these primitive agricultural tribes evolved into a single nation that embodied most of the elements of Egyptian civilization. By 3200 B.C., these early people had developed a highly complex written language; their craftsmen could fashion objects from the

In this illustration from a Book of the Dead, the jackal-headed funeral god Anubis weighs the heart of the dead man, before the throne of Osiris, god of the dead.

hardest stone, or delicate ornaments of great beauty from copper, wood, ivory; their architects had already undertaken the building of monumental structures. Five centuries later, their descendants were building gigantic pyramids nearly 500 feet high, carefully planned and of exquisite workmanship.

What had happened in so remarkably brief a period, that had transformed this group of semi-barbaric tribesmen into a highly civilized state that was to last for nearly 3000 years?

16

While there is no certain answer, the archaeological evidence gives us several clues. On pottery found at Gerza in Lower Egypt, dating back to about 3600 B.C., and later in scenes painted on mud-covered walls, there appear pictures of large boats. Since no timber for such vessels, especially for the tall masts, was to be found in Egypt, there must have been contact with the nearest timber-producing country —which was Lebanon, famous for its cedars. Further evidence was added when such wood was found lining the walls of some of the tombs of the Predynastic Period. This oriental influence was again indicated when certain objects were discovered, among them a knife on whose ivory handle are carved ships showing a crescent-shaped symbol, a typical feature of Mesopotamian vessels. On the reverse side of the handle, a bearded figure is shown standing between two rampant lions, a common motif on early Mesopotamian seals.

During the transitional period, the Egyptian tribesmen lived in much the same way as their forefathers had. They still worshiped animal gods and lived in small, separate agricultural groups along the river banks. Occasionally, several groups banded together to wage war upon a common enemy, and before 3200 B.C., powerful chieftains had arisen who celebrated their conquests on carved palettes of schist—

17

The carved handle of a flint knife found at Gebel el Araq shows warriors engaged in a river battle. The shape of the boats suggests a Mesopotamian influence upon the Predynastic Egyptian artisans.

enlarged and elaborate versions of the simple slate palettes that were buried in the little pit graves of earlier centuries. The discovery of these palettes along with carved knife handles and fine stone vessels provided unmistakable links between the primitive valley dwellers and the sophisticated Egyptians who lived under the rule of the great pharaohs.

The most dramatic of all these discoveries was made in 1898, in the temple of Hierakonpolis in Upper Egypt. There, archaeologists discovered a magnificent large palette which proved to be one of the most important historical documents ever found in Egypt. On one side of the palette is a figure wearing the Egyptian kilt that is so familiar in later representations. On his head is the tall crown of Upper Egypt; in one hand he grasps a mace while with the other, he grasps the hair of a kneeling figure, obviously representing an enemy. On the other side of the palette the same dominant figure wears the crown of Lower Egypt. On both sides is the hieroglyphic inscription "Narmer," enclosed in the symbolic design that indicates royalty.

The significance of this discovery was tremendous because here, for the first time, archaeological evidence could be linked with written records. For according to the Egyptian historian Manetho, who lived in the third century B.C., Upper and Lower Egypt were unified by a conqueror from the south, in about 3200 B.C. The name of this conqueror, in Greek, was Menes, whom scholars have identified as the first pharaoh, Narmer.

Manetho lived in Egypt during the rule of the Ptolemies. He compiled a list of Egyptian kings from the earliest known pharaohs, and he divided it into thirty-one different dynasties or ruling families.

Acrobatic dancers perform to the accompaniment of hand clapping in this relief. Their long hair is weighted so that it will swing behind them as they move.

Until about seventy years ago, no trace could be found of the twenty-six pharaohs that Manetho listed as rulers during the first three dynasties. Yet Manetho's references to the Fourth Dynasty were well substantiated by the magnificent monument of one of its pharaohs —the great Pyramid of Cheops. Obviously, there must have been a period of enormous activity between Predynastic Egypt and the time of Cheops, for the building of this monumental

In one Egyptian view of the universe, the sky goddess Nut, her body spangled with stars, is held high above the earth by Shu, the god of the air. Geb, the earth god and Nut's husband, lies exhausted at Shu's feet.

pyramid showed a degree of technology and civilization far beyond the reach and knowledge of the early tribal people of the Nile.

A series of dramatic discoveries, all made within a decade, finally provided confirmation of Manetho's lists. Narmer's palette proved beyond all doubt that the first king of the First Dynasty was no myth. At about the same time of this discovery, a French scholar, E. Amélineau, made excavations near Abydos, in Upper Egypt. There, he came upon a number of mud-brick tombs or *mastabas,* in which many fragments of jars, bits of ivory and other relics were scattered. On these fragments the names of a number of Egyptian kings were inscribed. Other archaeologists found more relics at the site, and scholars began to study the inscrip-

tions on the fragments. It was a dramatic moment when it was announced that here undoubtedly were actual records of some of Manetho's kings of the First and Second Dynasties, who had ruled Egypt at the dawn of her dynastic history.

Let us reconsider for a moment why one of the earliest and longest-lived civilizations of the world should have developed in Egypt. Certainly, geographical accident, and political unity that was first imposed by force, (and thereafter maintained by intelligent, farseeing rulers), were important factors. Another necessity for the creation of civilization is easy communication, which in Egypt was provided by the Nile. A third is fertile soil, in this case insured by the annual flooding of the Nile. A fourth vital element is some directing intelligence. Only men of high intellectual caliber and forceful character could have transformed a group of independent tribes into a single state. Narmer may have been such a man.

With the end of warfare among the tribes, the Egyptians needed only to exert an organized effort to make good use of the ample resources of the land. The Egyptian year was divided into the seasons beginning with the rise of the Nile, the "inundation," followed by the "emergence of the fields from the waters" (the period of cultivation), and then the "deficiency of water," the drought or harvest. When the swollen river flooded its banks, it covered the fields, spreading the rich silt borne down from the mountain heights by the waters of the Atbara and the Blue Nile. When the waters receded, all that was required was to hoe or plow shallow channels in the rich silt, plant crops, and wait for them to ripen.

Occasionally, there would be years when the flood was unusually low, and then famine would follow. In other times the great river would roar down in uncontrollable torrents, sweeping away men and beasts and the frail mud-brick buildings in its path. The Nile could bring life or death, prosperity or disaster. It was to this problem that the Egyptian intellectual class, its priest technicians, applied their minds.

Over the centuries, the Egyptians learned how to control the flood waters, to conserve them during the long dry season, and to preserve the precious top soil with a complex system of dikes and canals. Such a system could only be accomplished by large bodies of people working together, and this called for organization and discipline. The development of this intelligently directed communal effort marked an important step in the advance of Egyptian civilization.

The Third Dynasty started about 2670 B.C., ushering in Egypt's first golden age, known as the Old Kingdom. The era lasted through the Sixth Dynasty, for about 500 years. The pharaohs of this period enjoyed a concentration of power which, once lost, was never fully recovered. Their sculptured portraits are among the highest achievements of Egyptian art. It

21

Re-Harakhte, a composite god with the head of Horus the hawk, ruler of the heavens, and wearing Re's solar crown, receives the offerings of a worshiper.

was during this period that Egyptian architecture developed its most familiar and lasting form, the great pyramids, whose construction demanded such an enormous expenditure of wealth and labor.

Manetho notes briefly that it was one Imhotep who taught the Egyptians to build in stone. There is little other reference to the architect who must have been one of the great geniuses of Egypt. Imhotep was the vizier of Djoser, second pharaoh of the Third Dynasty. It was Imhotep who was responsible for raising the first great stone building on earth, the Step Pyramid at Saqqara. It remains the oldest,

22

most awe-inspiring monumental stone structure in the world.

The Step Pyramid was begun as a large stone *mastaba,* or tomb, for the pharaoh, Djoser. Later, Imhotep enlarged it by superimposing a number of progressively smaller stone mastabas on top of one another, thus finally achieving the form of a pyramid. Surrounded by smaller buildings and courts, the entire tomb area was once enclosed by a 34-foot wall which extended for more than a mile.

Djoser's pyramid, which faces within 1/20 of a degree of true north, was built of small stone blocks, little bigger than the mud bricks used in earlier mastabas. But within less than a century, huge blocks of white limestone were used. The Great Pyramid built for Pharaoh Cheops after 2600 B.C. used more than two million stone blocks, each weighing about two and a half tons. The main structure was over 750 feet along each base and rose to a height of nearly 500 feet. The stone blocks were cut so evenly that the blade of a knife could not be inserted between them when they were laid in place. Moreover, the giant granite stones had been quarried 600 miles away in Aswan and then brought by boat along the river. All this was achieved almost 5000 years ago by a people whose only mechanical devices were the lever, the roller, and the inclined plane.

Why did the Egyptians bury their pharaohs under millions of tons of stone, in richly adorned tombs? And why did they worship fantastic gods with human bodies and animal heads?

. The two principal religious cults at the time were those of Re, the sun god, and Osiris, god of death and resurrection. The sun is an ever-present force in Egypt, and it is easy to see why the Egyptians revered it as the giver of life. Every night, they believed, Re died in the west and every morning he was reborn in the east. It was doubtless for this reason that the Egyptians buried their dead in the west—indeed, one of their names for the dead was the "Westerners."

The cult of Osiris, his wife and sister Isis, and their son Horus, involves a myth: in the beginning, there was only a primeval ocean, upon which appeared an egg. From the egg, Re, the sun god was born. Re had four children—Geb, the earth god, Shu and Tefnut, gods of the atmosphere, and Nut, the sky goddess. In some Egyptian tombs, Nut is represented as a woman whose body is arched across the sky.

Osiris was the son of Geb and Nut, who also had three other children, Isis, Nephthys and Seth. Osiris married his sister Isis (within the Egyptian royal family brother-sister marriages were common), and later succeeded to the throne of Egypt. But his wicked brother Seth was jealous and plotted to kill him. This, Seth eventually did, and dismembered and scattered the parts of Osiris's body. Isis, however, recovered the parts of her husband's body, (all except the organ of generation), and with the help of the gods, reassembled and reanimated the corpse. But since Osiris had now lost his reproductive powers, he could no longer rule over the living. He therefore became god of the dead and judge of souls.

The second part of the myth concerns Osiris's and Isis's son Horus who sought out and slew Seth. After revenging his father, Horus himself ascended to the throne of Egypt.

The fact that this myth had such a strong hold on the Egyptian imagination was due, surely, to its humanity. While the cult of Re, the sun god, was rather austere, every wife could identify herself with the faithful Isis, and every son with Horus, every father with Osiris.

It is important to remember these myths for, from an early date, the Pharaoh was considered both god and king.

The ancient Egyptians believed in what we call the soul. In fact, they recognized two souls, the *ba* and the *ka,* which could survive in afterlife only if the body of the deceased was preserved and protected from harm. It was for this reason that they practiced mummification.

The embalming procedure was refined and improved over the years until it became a skilled art. The de luxe method, reserved for royalty and high officials, took several months. First the embalmers removed the viscera and placed them in a set of stone vessels, known as canopic jars. The heart, however, was reinserted in the body, probably because it was regarded as the seat of intelligence.

The eviscerated corpse was soaked in a bath of niter for about 70 days, after which it was dried and wrapped in resinous linen. Before the wrapping, however, the embalmer placed linen pads under the skin to fill out the sunken cheeks and to give the appearance of firmness to the limbs, which were then adorned with fine jewelry and ornaments.

In addition, the figure of the deceased was reproduced in sculptures and paintings, in order to provide other substitute refuges for the spirits. These likenesses, buried in the chambers of the dead, were not intended to be seen by living eyes. The main point was to preserve the appearance of the body so that the *ba* or *ka* would recognize it even if the mortal remains were destroyed. The dead also had to be provided with food, drink and other material needs of a living body.

Other peoples to our own day have also believed devoutly in an afterlife, but none have taken such elaborate precautions to assure life after death. We say, "You can't take it with you," but the Egyptians believed that they could. There was nothing morbid about their concept of death. Rather, it projected into the afterlife the busy, cheerful, and plentiful life that the Egyptian wanted to enjoy everlastingly.

Egyptians attached a magical value to representations of themselves and their possessions —their families and servants as well as their houses, gardens, flocks, and herds—whereby these paintings and models took on the attributes of the real thing, throughout eternity.

In representing his world, the ancient Egyptian artist observed certain fixed rules. Human figures were scaled according to their importance. Perspective as we know it was not attempted; nearer objects in a scene were depicted in the lower panels, while the more distant ones were shown in ascending order. In representing the human figure, artists showed the head in profile, but the eye appears in a frontal view. The torso is also seen from the front, but the arms and legs are in profile.

When the king died, his sepulcher was filled with rich furniture inlaid with ivory and gold, his chests of clothing, weapons, and ornaments. However, out of the more than 80 pyramids that were built, every one has long since been robbed of its precious possessions, leaving only the empty shells of the sacred tombs.

Some of the tombs of the pharaoh's noble courtiers have survived, however, and in some there are large reliefs showing scenes of the dead man's earthly life. Some show pictures of hunting, others, scenes of feasting. In these, we may see the nobleman and his wife seated on stately chairs, receiving their guests. Tables are spread with delicacies, servants pour wine, and dancing girls perform to the sound of flutes, harps, and drums. The food served at such banquets can be recognized from these paintings and sculptures. One such painting shows geese being artificially fattened for the vizier's table. Forced feeding of animals was quite common and is frequently depicted. *Pâté de foie gras* has a history of at least 5000 years.

Women are pictured sharing these social pleasures with their husbands. Frequently the couple are shown in an affectionate posture, the wife with her arm around her spouse. These ancient ladies have an elegance and sophistication which appeal to us, in an age when a slim, svelte line is again fashionable. They reddened their lips, painted their fingernails and toenails, and used heavy eye shadow. Just as modern carpenters, shown a set of Egyptian tools, would immediately recognize each of them, so also would a modern woman know what to do with most of the ancient Egyptian beauty aids.

The Step Pyramid of King Djoser, built during the Third Dynasty in the twenty-sixth century B.C., was the first of the great royal pyramids built and is the oldest monumental stone structure on earth.

Other tomb scenes show the sources of the wealth that supported this luxury. It came from the land. We see farm hands sowing and harvesting grain, and lines of fat cattle being driven to slaughter. On other tomb walls we see boys playing games. Sometimes hieroglyphic inscriptions present a line or two of dialogue. One highborn lady at a noble banquet cries out, "I want to drink until I'm drunk. My inside is like a straw," while a servant fills her goblet.

These tomb paintings allow us glimpses into the Egyptian past. Humble men and women are often depicted with compassion and humor, as also are the domestic animals. On the whole, it would appear that Egypt was governed both humanely and wisely.

Literacy was the first requirement for an official position. Being a scribe had many attractions, not the least of which was exemption from manual work. By about 2500 B.C., the Egyptians already had a growing body of literature. There were two methods of writing the language: the fully formed hieroglyphs which were usually carved in stone, and a flowing, cursive style with abbreviated symbols

which the Greeks later called hieratic. By extracting the pith from the papyrus reed, gluing the reeds together and drying them, the Egyptians produced a light, portable writing material upon which they wrote with fine brushes or rush pens. Our modern word *paper* is, of course, derived from *papyrus*.

Inscribed papyri found in Egyptian tombs include the earliest known medical text books; also, letters, state records, school exercise books, religious texts, stories and poems. Much of our knowledge of the ancient Egyptians is derived from these written accounts.

One of the most remarkable documents that has survived is the so-called Edwin Smith Papyrus, a copy of what was probably the earliest treatise on surgery. Another is the Rhind Papyrus, a famous mathematical document dealing with the problem of triangles.

Protected by the natural barriers of wastelands and the sea, Egypt developed and maintained its unique culture undisturbed by major foreign invasion over a period of some 2000 years. And it would appear that the Egyptian way of life seemed good to all concerned.

The priest Ka-aper lived at the beginning of the Fifth Dynasty after high government positions became available to men of non-royal blood.

EGYPT

2: rebellion and recovery

The pyramids that were built during the Fifth Dynasty were smaller and less carefully constructed than those of the preceding dynasty. They suggest a decline of the royal power, and when the absolute authority that had been exercised by the early kings diminished, rebellion and anarchy arose in some parts of the land. By the end of the Sixth Dynasty, Egypt was in a state of unrest and confusion, and the Old Kingdom came to an end.

How did it happen that the mighty pharaohs lost their supreme control over the land? As trade and commerce grew beyond Egypt's borders, the country's frontiers were governed by powerful border lords. Extension of power meant delegation of authority. Possibly there was the traditional conflict between the efficient frontier soldier, familiar with local conditions and problems, and the well-cushioned civil servants who issued the king's orders from the capital, hundreds of miles away. Gradually, the provincial governors, called nomarchs, became stronger and more independent and, as their power grew, they took for themselves

OVERLEAF: *Small models discovered in the tomb of Meketre, a Middle Kingdom noble, show the landowner counting cattle for the annual tax inspection.*

some of the privileges formerly reserved only for the king. They no longer built their tombs alongside the royal pyramid as their forefathers had done, but constructed them in their own districts. The next step was to decorate their tombs with painted offerings in the belief that they, like the Pharaoh, might join the gods in the afterworld. Subsequently, all Egyptians assumed this comforting privilege.

The participation of the common people in the cult of Osiris, the religion once reserved exclusively for the Pharaoh, brought about a profound change in Egyptian society. During the growth of the cult of the god of the dead, little statuettes called shawabtys were made. These little figures were supposed to represent the deceased, not as he appeared in life, but wrapped as a mummy. While the original function of the tomb sculptures was to provide a haven for the spirit if the actual body of the deceased were destroyed, the shawabty gradually assumed the character of a magic servant who took over all the hard or unpleasant tasks that might be demanded of the deceased by the gods in the hereafter.

Now, also, the cult of the sun god Re changed, as a minor deity named Amen began to be worshiped along with him. The center of Amen worship was the town of Thebes in Upper Egypt, and it was from this town that a new dynasty of pharaohs arose. In Thebes,

ABOVE, *a carpenter saws a board in half while two others work on a wooden beam with mallet and chisel.*

BELOW, *the lady Kawit holds a mirror and sips from a cup while a hairdresser attends to her coiffure.*

OPPOSITE, *female musicians perform on the lute, harp, and double flute. Women of the harem were called upon to dance or serenade the guests at banquets given by the royal court or by the rich men of the realm.*

provincial nomarchs won battles with neighboring areas, and with their victories, won also the right to rule a reunited Egypt. Thus began Egypt's second golden age, called the Middle Kingdom, which was ruled from 2133 to 1625 B.C. by the kings of the Eleventh and Twelfth Dynasties.

The statuary and the literature of the Middle Kingdom show some striking contrasts with those of the Old Kingdom. Portrait sculptures of the Old Kingdom show the rulers as idealized, aloof, even youthful figures far superior to ordinary mortals. Royal sculptures of the

A boat model, perhaps of a pleasure yacht, shows the crew working rudders and hoisting the sails.

Twelfth Dynasty show a far greater degree of naturalness, and the faces of many of the figures bear the marks of age and suffering. The times were not easy, as the pharaohs of these dynasties struggled to re-establish royal supremacy over rebellious nobles. Treachery was common and the reigning monarch had constantly to be on guard against all men, even his own brothers.

In spite of rebellion and general unrest, some of the rulers of this period made remarkable achievements. Sesotris I pushed the Egyptian frontier southward into Nubia. Ammenemes II reopened and exploited the gold mines in Sinai, and Sesotris III completely broke the resistance of the landed nobility and later cut a vast channel for his warships through the granite walls of the First Cataract and completely subjugated the land of Nubia to the south.

Highly polished bronze made a woman's handmirror.

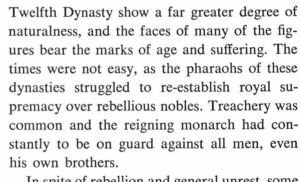

32

The tombs of the nobles of the Middle Kingdom have, like those of their predecessors, provided us with extraordinarily vivid records of the people and their ways of life. In 1920 Herbert Winlock, an American Egyptologist, made one of the most remarkable discoveries of recent times during his excavations at Thebes. While digging in the tomb of Meketre, a Middle Kingdom nobleman, Winlock came upon a little storeroom which had somehow miraculously escaped the robbers who plundered the tomb thousands of years ago. In the chamber were hundreds of little wooden models of men and women, made to represent the details of daily life of the nobleman and his servants.

An ointment spoon shows a girl swimming behind a duck whose wings conceal a compartment for perfume.

There were models of ships, ranging from a traveling boat whose crew were raising and trimming the sail, to smaller craft on which cooks were at work. These evidently followed the bigger vessel, in order to provide meals for the great man and his staff on their journey along the Nile. There were also models of faster ships, boats for hunting and fishing craft.

There were models of Meketre's residence with its pillared courtyard and trees surrounding an ornamental pool. Another model showed Meketre inspecting his cattle as they were driven past him, while he sat within a pillared pavilion. There was a model stable for his cattle, a butcher's shop, a granary, a brewery, a bakery, a weaving shop, a carpenter's shop—all teeming with tiny figures of the men and women who had served Meketre in life.

Like the paintings and reliefs described earlier, these little figures were designed to serve the needs of the dead man in the life to come.

Fortunately, many pieces of jewelry have also survived from the Middle Kingdom. The court jewelers of the Twelfth Dynasty had brought this ancient craft to an unsurpassed height of excellence. Many exquisite treasures, happily overlooked by ancient plunderers, were discovered by the archaeologist Jacques de Morgan in the late 19th century. Among them were diadems of delicate gold work with carnelian and lapis lazuli decorations. Some years later, Edwin Petrie, the English Egyptologist, uncovered an equally wonderful royal cache among which were a silver mirror, vases containing perfumed ointment and even small copper razors. There was a small girdle made of amethyst beads and golden shells, which made a tinkling sound when the wearer walked.

Among the pharaohs of the Middle Kingdom were men of great stature. But none of them enjoyed the absolute authority of the Old Kingdom rulers. With the end of the reign of Ammenemes III, the second great period of Egyptian history began to show signs of disintegration. In the Delta, the richest area in Egypt, there were indications of new turmoil. The region was nearest to the several foreign lands whose inhabitants, in times of unrest, were ever tempted to move in and settle in the land of the fertile Nile Valley.

LEFT, *the scribes, those men who understood how to read and write the language, often held positions of responsibility in the kingdom.*

ABOVE, *farm workers harvest the vineyards, picking the grapes and trampling them with their feet. In the lower panel, peasants net water birds in the marshes, and then clean and prepare them for the table.*

35

EGYPT

3: glory and decline

ACCORDING to Manetho, the Egyptian historian of the third century B.C., the Middle Kingdom ended after an "invasion" of Asiatic tribes whose leaders he called the Hyksos. These tribes originally came from Palestine, Lebanon, and Syria, and they could hardly be called invaders, for most of them had long since entered Egypt and had been settled in the Delta region for several generations.

Akhenaten, an Eighteenth Dynasty king, rebelled against Egypt's traditional religion, and with his wife Nefretiti, established his own cult of the sun disk.

An intelligent and energetic people, the Hyksos had provided a link with Western Asia and had brought with them many inventions from their homelands which were to have a great influence upon the more conservative Egyptians. Among these were the use of bronze for tools and weapons, and the powerful composite bow. They also introduced the horse, the wheel (almost unknown to the Egyptians before this period), and the horse-drawn war chariot.

Perhaps because they possessed superior weapons, the Hyksos were tempted to exploit

the weakness and dissension among Egypt's rulers, and to seize power in the Delta area. The Hyksos kings ruled for nearly 150 years during the so-called Second Intermediate Period, which lasted from 1786 to 1567 B.C. This was the first time in Egypt's long history that it was ruled by foreign kings.

However, during the late years of this Intermediate Period, a strong wave of nationalism arose among the Egyptians, and they gathered enough strength to turn upon the foreign intruders. Using the new kinds of weapons, and strategy that they had learned from the alien tribes, they were at last able to reunite Egypt under a native sovereign.

This sovereign was the Theban prince Sekenere, who with his successors Kamose and Ahmose, finally drove out the Asian tribes. When Ahmose succeeded to the throne in 1567 B.C., he founded the Eighteenth Dynasty, and with his reign, Egypt entered a period of unprecedented brilliance known to us as the New Kingdom. It was during this time that Egypt became established as the greatest and richest power on earth.

After ousting the Asiatic tribes from the Delta, the kings of the Eighteenth Dynasty carried their conquests into the homelands of the invaders, and thus, for the first time, they became conquerors and colonizers. For the first time also, thousands of Egyptians saw the countries that lay beyond their own sheltered valley.

A succession of pharaohs of the Eighteenth Dynasty extended Egypt's conquests far into Syria. The greatest of these rulers was Tuthmosis III, a proud and militant man who commissioned many works of art and literature in order to extol his victorious reign. Among these were many obelisks; tall, tapering pillars, one of which now stands in New York's Central Park, near the Metropolitan Museum. Three

Ruler of Egypt for seventeen years, Queen Hatshepsut built this immense temple at Thebes and imported myrrh trees from the south to decorate its terraces.

39

others stand in other major cities of the world, one on the Embankment in London, one in Istanbul, and one in Rome.

The conquests of Tuthmosis brought great wealth into Egypt—not only in war booty, but also in the form of taxation from the new colonies over which Egypt now ruled. Trade increased between the Nile Valley dwellers and the inhabitants of foreign lands, and with it, and with the drafting of foreign princes into service as rulers under the Egyptian flag, new influences filtered into the Egyptian culture. The pharaoh Amenhotep III brought foreign princesses back to his harem, and many other noble families took wives from among the foreign royalty.

Amenhotep's son, Amenhotep IV, is remembered chiefly for the short but remarkable religious revolution he initiated, along with his beautiful wife Nefretiti. The new religion was based on the idea of one god, called Aten, and represented by the sun's disk. Amenhotep changed his own name to Akhenaten, and tried to abolish all the other deities that had been worshiped by his countrymen. This religious revolution was reflected in a similar, and also shortlived revolution in art. Here, for the first time, painters and sculptors were encouraged to abandon the strict rules previously demanded, and to create their scenes and portraits as realistically as possible. Akhenaten himself was portrayed, not in a flattering, youthful, stylized manner, but apparently as he really was, with a heavy paunch, a long jaw, and rather effeminate features. He is also shown in informal postures, as a human and affectionate husband and father. Most famous of the sculptures of this period, however, is the well-known portrait bust of Nefretiti, now residing in a Berlin museum.

Akhenaten's rule was gentle and philosophical, and probably had little influence upon the majority of his subjects. After the pharaoh's death, Egypt returned to polytheism, her traditional worship of many gods. But Akhen-

Egyptian kings traditionally had themselves portrayed as absolute conquerors in war. Here, Tuthmosis III prepares to smite multitudes of bound Asiatics.

aten and his successors left a much more influential legacy behind them, for through neglect of imperial duties and Akhenaten's policy of pacifism, Egypt grew weaker at a time when a powerful new enemy, the Hittites of Asia Minor, were growing stronger and were pushing their conquests into Egypt's Syrian colonies.

The Eighteenth Dynasty came to a faltering close; but it was not long before a new dynasty came into power, and won back most of the territory lost by its predecessors. Two monarchs of this period, Sethi I and Ramesses II, commemorated their triumphs in inscriptions on the walls of the renovated temple of Amen-Re at Karnak. The enemy were still the Hittites, but once peace was signed, they were no longer called the "abominable Kheta;" now they were regarded as worthy allies and their leader as a great king.

Peace was shortlived after a treaty was signed with the Hittites, however. Fortunately for Egypt, she produced a pharaoh capable not only of ruling the sprawling empire but also of driving out new and even more treacherous invaders. Ramesses III of the Twentieth Dynasty was faced with hordes of new attackers who had swept out of their own lands north of the Mediterranean. Now they attacked by sea and land, swarming down the eastern coast of the Mediterranean seeking new lands.

Among these were the Philistines of biblical note, whom Ramesses met on land and at sea, and hurled back from the gates of Egypt. The victory went overwhelmingly to the Egyptians and the battles were commemorated in scenes on the temple walls at Medinet Habu.

The city of Thebes had long been the supreme capital of Egypt and in it, and in neighboring Karnak, great and magnificent buildings were erected as monuments to the power and prestige of the pharaohs who ruled from the city. The temple of Amen-Re at Karnak, enlarged and glorified by successive generations of pharaohs, became the largest religious building in the world, and none has ever been built

since that has exceeded it in size. The Hypostyle (or columned) Hall of this temple is almost as large as the whole of Canterbury Cathedral in England and it is just one of many rooms. Many of the 134 columns in the Hall are 12 feet thick and 69 feet high, and are crowned by capitals so large that 100 men could stand on

When Tutankhamen succeeded the heretic ruler Akhenaten, he restored to Egypt the worship of the god Amen, whose small gold statue is shown at left. The gilded lion, below left, decorated a funerary couch in Tutankhamen's tomb. The solid gold coffin below shows the young boy-king holding a crook and flail, which were Egyptian symbols of royalty.

them. The outer walls of the whole temple complex could easily enclose ten European cathedrals.

Stretching along the banks of the Nile were the palaces of the kings and the villas of the nobles. Here also were wharves for the ships loaded with goods from foreign ports, and the necropolis, or City of the Dead, which housed the tombs of kings and nobles. Here, too, against the Theban mountains, is the famous Valley of the Tombs of the Kings.

Because so many of the royal sepulchers had been looted by robbers seeking the riches buried within, architects now devised a new stratagem to protect them. Mastabas and pyramids were abandoned and instead, deep chambers were hewn into the limestone cliffs. Approached by long sloping corridors, the royal chambers were disguised by labyrinths of false hallways and rooms in order to baffle the tomb robbers. But as in the past, the robbers were able to negotiate even these tortuous passageways and to plunder nearly all of the tombs of the pharaohs of the New Kingdom.

Tomb robbery was risky, and made even more dangerous because it outraged Egyptian religious ideals. Even so, during the Twentieth Dynasty it became epidemic, for this was a time of stress, when there were many hungry and desperate men. But the thievery did at least restore a great deal of silver and gold into circulation at a time when Egypt sorely needed currency. With the ending of the Bronze Age and the begining of the use of iron, Egypt could no longer profit by mining the copper of the Sinai peninsula and manufacturing bronze for export. Now it had to import iron itself, for tools and weapons.

All of the pharaohs of the New Kingdom were buried in the Valley of the Kings. Yet only one tomb, a rather small one of a relatively minor pharaoh, Tutankhamen, survived the depredations of the grave robbers. Tutankhamen, a boy-king, reigning briefly at the end of the Eighteenth Dynasty, died when he was

not yet twenty years old. When his tomb was discovered by archaeologists in 1922, the world was astounded by the wealth which had lain hidden in the mountain fastness for over a hundred generations. The coffin in which the king's body lay was made of solid gold, and this was nested within outer coffins of richly ornamented wood. In adjoining chambers were the king's chariot and hunting gear, couches, chests, beds, clothing, ebony and ivory caskets, and jewelry of exquisite workmanship. Gold-plated statues and vases, toys and ornaments were nearby, and on the head of the body itself was a portrait mask of solid gold. All of this treasure was contained in four small chambers, one of the smallest of the royal tombs. One can only speculate on the riches that must have been hidden in the tombs of the great pharaohs such as Tuthmosis III or Ramesses II and III.

Most of these treasures are now housed in the Egyptian Museum in Cairo, as are also the bodies of some of the great pharaohs which, while stripped of their possessions, remained intact over a period of some 3000 years. Sekenere is there, as are Tuthmosis II and Sethi I, and the mighty Ramesses II.

After the end of the New Kingdom, Egypt underwent a long, slow period of decline, down to the fourth century B.C. None of the kings of this time ever attained the wealth and power of the pharaohs of the New Kingdom, and occasionally the native rule was interrupted by that of foreign conquerors. During this period of decline, the influence of the priests, always important in Egyptian life, gradually increased. Eventually, the high priest of Amen ruled the southern half of the Nile Valley from Thebes, while in the north, a merchant dynasty controlled the Delta region. More and more, earthly matters were decided upon by consultation with the oracles of the gods, with the priests interpreting the answers. Thus, the priests actually shared sovereignty with the king. Ritual now became fanatically important. In earlier ages, animals had been worshiped as manifestations of the gods. Now they were revered for themselves, carefully tended during their lifetimes and even mummified after death. Cats and crocodiles especially enjoyed this esteem, and whole cemeteries were set aside for their bodies.

Egyptian chronicles rarely mention the Jews, and it is uncertain under which pharaoh Moses lived. Many scholars date the Exodus in the 13th century B.C.; it seems likely that the Jews left about the time of Ramesses II. About 300 years later, Sheshonk, first king of the Twenty-second Dynasty, invaded Palestine and Judaea in 945 B.C., and it may have seemed as if Egypt were about to reassert her imperial power. However, the Assyrians and Babylonians had grown in strength so that they now enjoyed the prestige once held by Egypt alone. Egyptian troops, being largely composed of foreign mercenaries, were not united by patriotism,

Soldiers of the pharaoh, Egyptian lancers and Nubian bowmen march together in a group of wooden models representing an Eleventh Dynasty squadron.

and their weapons and military leadership were inferior to those of other nations. Between 715 and 300 B.C.; Egypt was occupied on and off by foreign rulers—the Kushites, the Assyrians, the Persians, and the Macedonians. Yet, during a century of the Twenty-sixth Dynasty, native Egyptians ruled the land and there was an attempted revival of the art and literature of the Old Kingdom.

During this century, the Greeks began to enter Egypt as traders and merchants, and they marveled at the power and persistence of the ancient culture. In the writings of Herodotus we can understand the wonder and respect with which he and his countrymen regarded the Egyptian colossus.

A hundred years later, the Ptolemies came to Egypt and founded its last dynasty. The last Ptolemy was Cleopatra, and when she died she did so with a dramatic and symbolic gesture, for the "asp" by whose bite she was killed was the royal cobra of Egypt, the symbol that Egyptian pharaohs had worn on their crown since the beginning of dynastic history.

In Egyptian art, the bull often symbolized Pharaoh. The carving above is part of a slate palette and shows a royal bull goring an enemy. Below the bull, the lion standing within a walled fortress represents a captured town.

Two Reports

from

Contemporary

Observers

IN THE THIRD CENTURY B.C., THE GREEK HISTORIAN HERODOTUS WROTE OF THE MARVELS HE HAD SEEN ON HIS EXTENSIVE TRAVELS IN EGYPT:

". . . more monuments which beggar description are to be found (in Egypt) than anywhere else in the world. . . . Not only is the Egyptian climate peculiar to that country, and the Nile different in its behavior from other rivers elsewhere, but the Egyptians themselves in their manners and customs seem to have reversed the ordinary practices of mankind. For instance, women attend market and are employed in trade, while men stay at home and do the weaving. In weaving the normal way is to work the threads of the weft upward, but the Egyptians work them downward. Men in Egypt carry loads on their heads, women on their shoulders . . . no woman holds priestly office, either in the service of goddess or god; only men are priests in both cases. . . . In other nations the relatives of the deceased in time of mourning cut their hair, but the Egyptians, who shave at all other times, mark a death by letting the hair grow both on head and chin. They live with their animals—unlike the rest of the world, who live apart from them. . . . In writing or calculating, instead of going, like the Greeks, from left to right, the Egyptians go from right to left—and obstinately maintain that theirs is the dexterous method, ours being left-handed and awkward. They have two sorts of writing, the sacred and the common. They are religious to excess, beyond any other nation in the world, and here are some of the customs which illustrate the fact: they drink from brazen cups which they scour every day—everyone, without exception. They wear linen clothes which they make a special point of continually washing. . . . (The priests) bathe in cold water twice a day and twice every night—and observe innumerable other ceremonies besides. Their life, however, is not by any means all hardship, for they enjoy advantages, too; for instance, they are free from all personal expense, having bread made for them out of the sacred grain; and a plentiful supply of goose meat and beef, with wine in addition. Fish they are forbidden to touch; and as for beans, they cannot even bear to look at them because they imagine they are unclean. . . . Bulls are considered the property of the god Epaphus—or Apis—and are therefore tested in the following way: a priest appointed for the purpose examines the animal, and if he finds even a single black hair upon him, pronounces him unclean; he goes over him with the greatest care. . . . He also inspects the tail to make sure the hair on it grows properly; then, if the animal passes all these tests successfully, the priest marks him by twisting round his horns a band of papyrus which he seals with wax and stamps with his signet ring. The bull is finally taken away, and the penalty is death for anybody who sacrifices an animal which has not been marked in this manner. . . .

"All Egyptians use bulls and bull-calves for sacrifice, if they have passed the test for "cleanness"; but they are forbidden to sacrifice cows, on the ground that they are sacred to Isis. The statues of Isis show a female figure with cow's horns, like the Greek representations of Io, and of all animals cows are universally held by the Egyptians in the greatest reverence. This is the reason why no Egyptian, man or woman, will kiss a Greek, or use a Greek knife, spit, or caldron, or even eat the flesh of a bull known to be clean, if it has been cut with a Greek knife."

THE BUILDING OF THE PYRAMIDS: "Up to the time of Rhampsinitus, Egypt was excellently governed and very prosperous; but his successor Cheops . . . brought the country into all sorts of misery.

Amenhotep III ruled Egypt when the empire stood at the peak of its power. A cosmopolitan pharaoh with a taste for extravagant building projects, he had built, beside his funerary temple near Thebes, two giant statues of himself, later called the Colossi of Memnon.

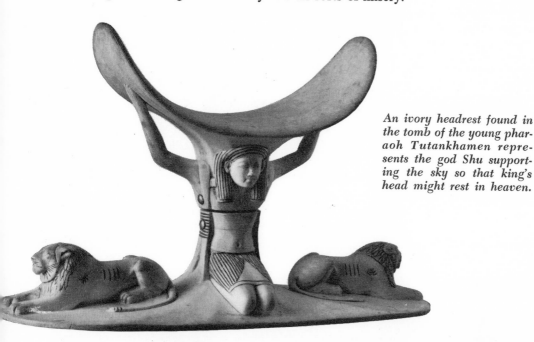

An ivory headrest found in the tomb of the young pharaoh Tutankhamen represents the god Shu supporting the sky so that king's head might rest in heaven.

47

The so-called "palette of Narmer" shows the first king of Egypt, the man who united the Nile Valley into one empire. Here he wears the white crown of Upper Egypt; the reverse side of the palette shows him wearing the red crown of Lower Egypt.

He closed all the temples, then, not content with excluding his subjects from the practice of their religion, compelled them without exception to labor as slaves for his own advantage. Some were forced to drag blocks of stone from the quarries in the Arabian hills to the Nile, where they were ferried across and taken over by others, who hauled them to the Libyan hills. The work went on in three-monthly shifts, a hundred thousand men in a shift. It took ten years of this oppressive slave-labor to build the track along which the blocks were hauled—a work, in my opinion, of hardly less magnitude than the pyramid itself. . . . To build the pyramid took twenty years; it is of polished stone blocks beautifully fitted, none of the blocks being less than thirty feet long. The method employed was to build it in tiers, or steps, if you prefer the word . . . when the base was complete, the blocks for the first tier above it were lifted from ground level by cranes or sheerlegs, made of short timbers; on this first tier there was another lifting-crane, which raised the blocks a stage higher, then yet another which raised them higher still. . . . An inscription is cut upon (the pyramid) in Egyptian characters recording the amount spent on radishes, onions, and leeks for the laborers, and I remember distinctly that the interpreter who read me the inscription said that the sum was sixteen hundred talents of silver. If this is true, how much must have been spent in addition on bread and clothing for the laborers during all those years the building was going on—not to mention the time it took to quarry and haul the stone, and to construct the underground chamber?

ANIMALS, SACRED AND FORBIDDEN: "Some Egyptians reverence the crocodile as a sacred beast, others do not, but treat it as an enemy. . . . in Thebes and around Lake Moeris . . . they keep one particular crocodile, which they tame, putting rings made of glass or gold into its ears and bracelets round its front feet, and giving it special food and ceremonial offerings. In fact, while these creatures are alive they treat them with every kindness, and when they die, embalm them and bury them in sacred tombs. On the other hand, in the neighborhood of Elephantine, crocodiles are not considered sacred animals at all, but are eaten. . . .

The hippopotamus is held sacred in the district of Papremis, but not elsewhere. This animal has four legs, cloven hoofs like an ox, a snub nose, a horse's mane and tail, conspicuous tusks, a voice like a horse's neigh, and is about the size of a very large ox. Its hide is so thick and tough that when dried it can be made into spearshafts.

EGYPTIAN TRADITION: "The Egyptians who live in the cultivated parts of the country, by their practice of keeping records of the past, have made themselves much the best historians of any nation of which I have had experience. . . . The Egyptians keep to their native customs and never adopt any from abroad."

THE SICILIAN WRITER DIODORUS BEGAN HIS HISTORY OF THE WORLD, WRITTEN IN THE FIRST CENTURY B.C., WITH THE STORY OF EGYPT, "SINCE EGYPT IS THE COUNTRY WHERE MYTHOLOGY PLACES THE ORIGIN OF THE GODS."

EGYPT'S POPULATION AND WEALTH: "In density of population it far surpassed all known regions of the inhabited world, and even in our own day is thought to be second to none other; . . . in ancient times it had over eighteen thousand important villages and cities. . . . The total population was . . . about seven million and the number has remained no less down to our day. . . .

Since the Nile has a gentle current, carries down a great quantity of all kinds of earth, and, furthermore, gathers in stagnant pools in low places, marshes are formed which abound in every kind of plant . . . tubers of every flavor grow in them and fruits and vegetables which grow on stalks . . . supplying an abundance sufficient to render the poor and the sick among the inhabitants self-sustaining . . . most of the children are reared without shoes or clothing because of the mildness of the climate of the country, the entire expense incurred by the parents of a child until it comes to maturity is not more than twenty drachmas. . . .

A MONUMENT TO RAMESSES II: "Ten stades from the first tombs . . . stands a monument of the king known as Osymandyas . . . beside the entrance are three statues, each of a single block of black stone from Syene, of which one, that is seated, is the largest of any in Egypt, the foot measuring over seven cubits. . . . And it is not merely for its size that this work merits approbation, but it is also marvelous by reason of its artistic quality and excellent because of the nature of the stone, since in a block of so great a size there is not a single crack or blemish to be seen. The inscription upon it runs: 'King of Kings am I, Osymandyas. If anyone would know how great I am and where I lie, let him surpass one of my works.' "

ROBBERY IN EGYPT: "The Egyptian law dealing with thieves was also a very peculiar one. For it bade any who chose to follow this occupation to enter their names with the Chief of Thieves and by agreement to bring to him immediately the stolen articles, while any who had been robbed filed with him in like manner a list of all the missing articles, stating the place, the day, and the hour of the loss. And since by this method all lost articles were readily found the owner who had lost anything had only to pay one-fourth of its value in order to recover just what belonged to him. For as it was impossible to keep all mankind from stealing, the lawgiver devised a scheme whereby every article lost would be recovered upon payment of a small ransom."

Toueris, the pregnant hippopotamus, was considered by the ancient Egyptians to be both a symbol of fertility and a goddess who watched over childbirth. In another role, she was also a patroness of vengeance. Bastet, the cat goddess of joy, also guarded against disease. Anubis, the god of the cemetery, appears here in the form of a jackal.

MESOPOTAMIA

1. sumer and the dawn of civilization

THE world's earliest civilization arose some six thousand years ago in the marshlands of Sumer in southern Mesopotamia. This is in the eastern part of the "fertile crescent," an area of south-western Asia that stretches from Palestine on the Mediterranean, around northern Arabia to the Persian Gulf. Most of the eastern half of the crescent, lying between the Tigris and the Euphrates Rivers, falls within the territory of modern-day Iraq.

Made of gold foil and lapis, the bull's head at left decorates the sound box of a harp found in the Royal Cemetery of the ancient Sumerian city of Ur.

Today, the landscape is a desolate one, a long flat valley of dried alluvial mud. The brown plains give way in the north to the stony uplands of Armenia. In and around this valley, long before the classic age of Greece, were the great empires of Assyria and Babylonia. And here, more than two thousand years still earlier, the Sumerians developed a remarkable civilization which is the first one known on earth.

By 7000 B.C., primitive peoples who lived on the fringes of this region had begun to gather crops, and to farm the land. Archaeologists have discovered the settlements of these early farmers in many areas, in Iran, Iraq, and south-

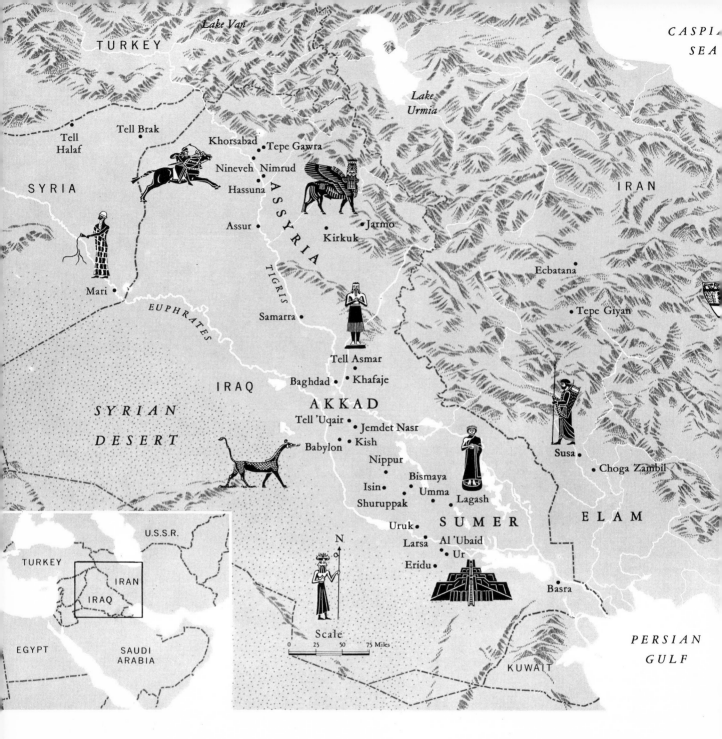

The world's first civilization was born in the land between the Tigris and the Euphrates Rivers. Here, Sumer, Akkad, and Assyria grew, and here, the great cities of Ur, Lagash, Nippur, Babylon, and Nineveh flourished.

eastern Turkey. One such settlement is at Qalat Jarmo, in the grassy uplands of northern Iraq. From about 7000 B.C., Jarmo was occupied by a succession of primitive agricultural communities whose farmers used flint-bladed sickles to reap their grain; they domesticated goats, and possibly dogs, too. Their homes were built of bricks made of pressed mud.

Jarmo is one of the most ancient settlements in Mesopotamia. Other sites, probably built from 5500 to 4000 B.C., have also been discovered. All were the settlements of primitive hunter-farmers who gradually moved into the Tigris-Euphrates Valley, seeking more desirable land. There is no historical record of these movements, except in legend, but a scientific examination of the sites has revealed a fascinating story.

At Hassuna in northern Iraq, archaeologists have been able to trace the development of a town from the time when primitive man first camped there down through the centuries to the days when he had begun to make substantial buildings. In the bottom layer of the diggings at the site, next to the virgin soil, excavators found a camp strewn with tools of stone and bone, crude pottery containers, and clay pellets for use in slings; but there was no trace of any dwelling. Here, perhaps, a group of nomads had moved down from the mountains and camped on the fertile grasslands at the junction of two streams. Perhaps they were attracted by the abundance of fish and game, and the possibility of reaping a crop of wild barley before the winter storms forced them to move on. Later, when they returned, they found that the trees were again bearing fruit, and there was more wild barley. In time the idea would occur that they might settle here and build some form of protection against the winter.

This appears to be just what happened. In the next stage uncovered by the excavations, the nomads had learned to sow the crops which they had seen growing there. Later still, mud huts appeared, and better pottery, until at last, near the top layer of the mound, were the remains of a complete agricultural community, hardly different from the nearby twentieth century village of Hassuna. At about 4000 B.C., however, the prehistoric Hassuna seems to have been abandoned.

Such a story as this, based purely on layers of pottery fragments, mud-brick foundations, and primitive tools, is as stirring as the legend of creation, for here indeed is "Man in the making." And further, there is no doubt that the descendants of these people built the great Sumerian cities with their high ziggurats, or temple towers, invented writing, and developed mathematics and astronomy, creating a

culture that lasted down to the time of the classical Greeks. Again and again in the mountains north and east of Mesopotamia, archaeologists have found the remains of similar communities. Through the artifacts, especially the pottery, they have been able to trace the progress of their culture into the river valley.

It is not easy for the layman to understand how important pottery is to the archaeologist. The history of mankind as revealed by archaeology alone, without the aid of written records, is largely a history of technology and artifacts. Pottery is the most common of these artifacts, and its value lies in the fact that it provides a trade mark by which we can follow the development and spread of a particular culture.

Neolithic settlements like those at Hassuna were followed by others of a people called the Tell Halaf folk, who lived for many centuries in the hills and northern plains of Mesopotamia. Later, in the south, a new wave of migrants entered the river valley from the highlands of Iran. These, the al 'Ubaid people, were farmers and stock breeders, and were

The victory of Lagash over one of its neighbors was commemorated on a stele which showed the deity of the city holding the enemy in a net, bludgeoning one of them with his mace.

Grandson of the first Semitic ruler of Mesopotamia, Naram-sin took as his own title King of the Four Quarters of the World. The pink sandstone sculpture below shows him wearing the horned helmet of the gods and standing over two foes while others plead for mercy. His own men follow him up a mountain slope.

skilled in many crafts. They used both stone and flint implements, and produced greenish pots of many shapes, decorated with designs in black paint.

The great leaders of later times were fortunate in being born after the invention of writing, and at a time when they were able to leave permanent memorials. The early leaders of these primitive nomadic farmers have left no record, but they must have existed, if only for the reason that in historical times, we know that important advances are usually initiated by such gifted and forceful people, and seldom by accident or circumstances alone.

At the site of the ancient city of Eridu, excavators have found the remains of large temples which date from the al 'Ubaid period, about 4000 to 3500 B.C. But in the following Uruk period, from 3800 to 3200 B.C., there was extensive building of monumental architecture and the development of the first real cities. The sacred buildings in Uruk were colorfully decorated with mosaic patterns made of clay cones dipped in pigment. At another site, there were wall paintings showing processions of human and animal figures. This richness of decoration, no less than the size of the buildings, provides impressive testimony to the level of accomplishment reached in the land of Sumer as early as the fourth millennium B.C.

But the people of Uruk may be given credit for an even more important innovation, the development of writing. For at this time we find the first primitive pictographs from which the cuneiform system of writing evolved.

The first writing probably developed through the necessity for keeping records. When people began to live together in large and complex social groups, and were faced with the problems of accumulating, storing, and distributing surplus wealth, the need for a permanent and accurate system of remembering things became urgent.

The first examples of writing are lists of objects: so many head of cattle, so many jars of oil, so many captives. Most of the earliest writing symbols were pictures—a cow's head, a man or a woman, a wine jar, a sword or a shield, the disk of the sun or moon. Thus an exchange of goods could be recorded by picturing a number of cows and, perhaps in exchange, a number of jars. Moons might indicate the length of time over which the bargain was to be made. Later the pictographs gave way to a series of signs which were easier to write; they no longer represented objects, but were symbols of the sounds of human speech. Numbers were, of course, also written, by a series of dots or strokes. Thus writing was born.

The Sumerians wrote on the same material they used for their buildings—mud. Nearly all Mesopotamian writings are on clay tablets, usually about the size of a postcard. Thousands of these tablets, although fragile, have survived. It is from the tablets, far more than the spectacular ziggurats, temples, and palaces, that we can trace the history of each of the successive Mesopotamian civilizations.

Unlike Egypt, which was protected from outside intrusion by natural barriers, (mountainous cliffs, hundreds of miles of formidable desert sands, and the Mediterranean Sea), Mesopotamia's flat valley land provided no natural defenses. The fertile plains and valleys were an open invitation to new settlers, and attracted both migrants and conquerors who, time and again, spread across the land over a period of many generations. Despite such frequent invasions, however, the basic pattern of civilization that had been established by the Sumerians remained fairly constant.

Before 2500 B.C. Sumer was occupied by a number of city-states. There was no central authority, as in Egypt, and the earliest governments were primitive democracies ruled by assemblies of all the adult men (excepting, of course, the slaves). In times of crisis, however, the assemblies would elect a king to whom they gave absolute authority for the duration of the emergency. While this was originally a tem-

The Royal Cemetery at Ur revealed this gay and elaborate headdress made of silver, gold, and lapis.

porary expedient, it later became permanent, as social relations between the states grew more complex and threatening.

In southern Mesopotamia, the land was extremely fertile because of the river-borne mud. But as in Egypt, it was necessary to control the flow of the rivers in order to farm the land usefully. Thus, a large-scale plan of irrigation was developed. An elaborate system of canals conserved the water brought down by winter floods, and the land was then able to support a large and growing population.

As it became easier to grow crops and to feed the livestock, it was no longer necessary for everyone to use all of their time producing food. Thus freed, some men were able to devote their energies to other matters, and so became priests, carpenters, metal-workers, and so on. The most important of these, of course, were the priests and rulers who governed and protected the land. It was they who could interpret the mysterious and terrifying forces of the sun, rain, flood, and tempest which brought abundance or famine, wealth or poverty, and which produced fertility or sterility in men, cattle or crops. These were the wise men who understood how the earth began, and how natural forces kept it in balance.

Next in importance to this intellectual group were the administrators and civil servants, the scribes who had learned how to write and who kept records of crop yields, flood levels, annual returns from taxation, the movement of the stars, and the achievements of their great men. Below these officials were the architects and builders, the artisans and carpenters, boatmen and jewelers. The spinners and weavers were usually slaves and in the lowest social rank. A fourth and most important group were the merchants and traders who brought in sorely needed commodities from the outside world.

There were many Sumerian cities along the Tigris and the Euphrates, such as Eridu, Khafaje, Lagash, Shuruppak, Uruk, Nippur, and Ur, the city where according to tradition, Abraham the patriarch was born. Buildings in these cities were made of mud bricks, and each town was surrounded by a defensive wall. At Khafaje, there was a series of interior walls, graduated in height, surrounding the temple at the center of the city. Within these walls there were houses and shops, stores and warehouses.

Around the city were fertile fields and vineyards; dominating each locality was the temple of the chief deity, usually placed on a high mound of earth. One such temple discovered at Uruk, and probably constructed in the fourth millennium B.C., had its shrine rising from a platform that was forty feet high. Later, these sacred temple towers were built to enormous heights, and like the pyramids, must have cost millions of hours of labor. Unlike the pyramids, however, they were not tombs. Their purpose

These stone figurines, perhaps representing a god and goddess and their worshipers, indicate the awe and dependence the Sumerians felt toward their gods.

This mosaic, called the "Standard," was found in the
Royal Cemetery at Ur, adorning one side of a box. It
appears to represent a victory celebration; the king,
seated in the upper left register facing his men, drinks

with them and listens to a musician playing on a bull's head harp. The middle register shows bulls, rams, and fish being brought to the banquet table; at bottom are teams of captured onagers, and porters carrying booty.

was simply to bridge the gap between man and god. A temple at the top of the tower was to serve as a welcome chamber for the god descending from heaven. At ground level, another chamber was provided for the deity during his stay on earth. A long stairway linked the two chambers—bringing to mind Jacob's vision of the "ladder" that reached to heaven, on which he saw "the angels of god ascending and descending."

There is no real modern equivalent of these ancient temples, for religion to the Sumerians was not a separate moral or spiritual concept, but was an immediate and constant part of their lives. The god or goddess of the city was the core of its existence, and all of the community life was devoted to the interests of the temple.

Gods and demons controlled every aspect of life. All natural forces were personified by one deity or another, who, having the power of life or death over men, had constantly to be propitiated. According to legend, the Sumerians had been created to live as serfs on the estates of the gods. And the Sumerians found their divine masters as unpredictable as human ones.

The gods could be angry, vengeful or selfish, and occasionally compassionate. Like human beings, they appreciated good food and wine, fine clothing and other luxuries. They married, had children, and sometimes quarreled among themselves. To all the Sumerians, of all classes, these deities were as real as the king and the priests who administered the estates of the gods.

Every Sumerian was equal before the gods. In the earliest period, all men had been assigned tasks to perform as divine service, and all were given rations from the temple storeroom, and allotments of land which they could farm for themselves. Eventually, this system developed divisions of labor and class distinctions. The economy of the Sumerian temple com-

Around 2300 B.C., Sargon of Akkad brought all the Sumerian city-states under his rule. The bronze head at left is thought to portray this great Semitic king.

munity has been termed a system of theocratic socialism. Yet from an early date, personal ownership of wealth was recognized and there were ample opportunities for private enterprise.

An extraordinary and touching example of the Sumerian spirit of collective devotion was found in the death pits of Ur, discovered by Leonard Woolley in 1923. Near the walls of the city, Woolley came upon a cemetery containing nearly two thousand graves. Among these were sixteen which clearly belonged to distinguished personages. Within each stone sepulcher lay a body, male or female, in full costume of gold, silver, and semi-precious stones. In the deep pits surrounding the stone chambers or on the sloping ramps that approached them, were the bodies of scores of men, women, and animals. In one pit, there were sixty-eight women, all of whom had been buried in red woolen robes, with headdresses of gold or silver. Some of the women had musical instruments such as lyres or harps made of wood and ornamented with gold, silver, shell, lapis lazuli, and red stone. They were probably court musicians. The wood in their instruments had decayed, but its impression had remained in the soil, so archaeologists, by taking wax casts, were able to reconstruct them. The gold and silver mountings were replaced, and they now may be seen in the British Museum, London, in all their original beauty. The decorations were most commonly fashioned in the form of an animal's head, that of a cow, or a magnificently bearded bull. In one case, the whole figure of a stag is shown.

In another pit grave, Woolley found soldiers in copper helmets, their spears at their sides. The bodies were lying in orderly rows, giving the impression that these people had met a peaceful death. The little cups that lay beside them may have contained poison or a drug. These people may have been alive when they entered the pits and were, perhaps self-sacrificed. It would appear, at least, that they went to their deaths calmly, without fuss.

61

The Sumerians, however, did not view death and the hereafter with the confidence of the Egyptians. According to passages from certain Sumerian poems, they had no such thought of a better world to come. One description relates that,

". . . . the Dead shuffle
Under their black plumage . . . where the food is
clay
And they drink ashes . . . . whence there is no re-
prieve."

Yet the evidence suggests that these well-dressed ladies and gentlemen of 4500 years ago went quietly to their graves. No signs of violence are there to intimate that they were forced into the pits. It seems likely, rather, that they allowed themselves to be sacrificed because they believed it to be a religious duty necessary for the city-state, which could be preserved only by the sacrifice of a king and his retainers. Such a custom is described in epic poetry of the period, and it has its parallels in numerous ancient societies.

What is clear from the Ur tombs is the wealth and beauty and fine craftsmanship of the period. The quality of the workmanship is highly sophisticated and is comparable to the best Egyptian work of the same period. One of the women's headdresses is as absurdly delightful as a modern Paris hat, and the gold and lapis figure of a goat standing on its hind legs has often been compared to the biblical "ram in a thicket"; an electrum helmet faithfully reproduces the intricate male hairdo of Sumerian fashion.

Little scenes are depicted on the sides of musical instruments. On the famous "Ur Standard," Sumerian soldiers march in step, spears ready, driving captured enemy prisoners before them. The king's chariot, a heavy-wheeled affair, is drawn by wild asses. On the other side of the "Standard" are peaceful scenes of the king and his nobles feasting, while a musician plays on his harp.

These representations do not show the Sumerians as a particularly handsome people, for they appear with stocky figures, hooknosed faces, and a general lack of animation. Unlike the stylized character of Egyptian art, early Mesopotamian art varied from extreme realism to abstraction. The head of a bull from a harp found at Ur conveys to perfection the animal vitality of its subject. And the famous Warka Head of a woman (Warka is the modern name for ancient Uruk), is subtly modeled, with serene grace, and might almost have come from classical Greece.

There are also a great many little carved cylinders of stone or metal which were used for sealing documents. They are engraved with such delicacy that we can hardly believe they were executed without the aid of a magnifying glass. Used to seal inscribed tablets, they were also used to identify and protect property. They were rolled over pats of moist clay that covered the fastenings of jar and basket tops. After the impression dried and hardened, the container could not be opened without damaging the sealing.

The scenes depicted on the cylinder seals are always religious in nature. In some we can recognize a familiar figure often thought to be the epic hero Gilgamesh, grappling with monsters, slaying two lions with his bare hands, and, with his companion Enkidu, performing other feats that are described in the famous Sumerian epic.

Thousands of seals have been recovered, so they probably represented a form of art that persisted over a long period of time. They are the only objects that have survived in sufficient quantity to provide a comprehensive view of Mesopotamian art over the ages. They were usually attached to a necklace or wristband and were worn to the grave by their owners.

In the Early Dynastic period of Mesopotamia, from 3000 to 2370 B.C., great palaces as large as the temples were built in the Sumerian cities. The land was subjected to repeated

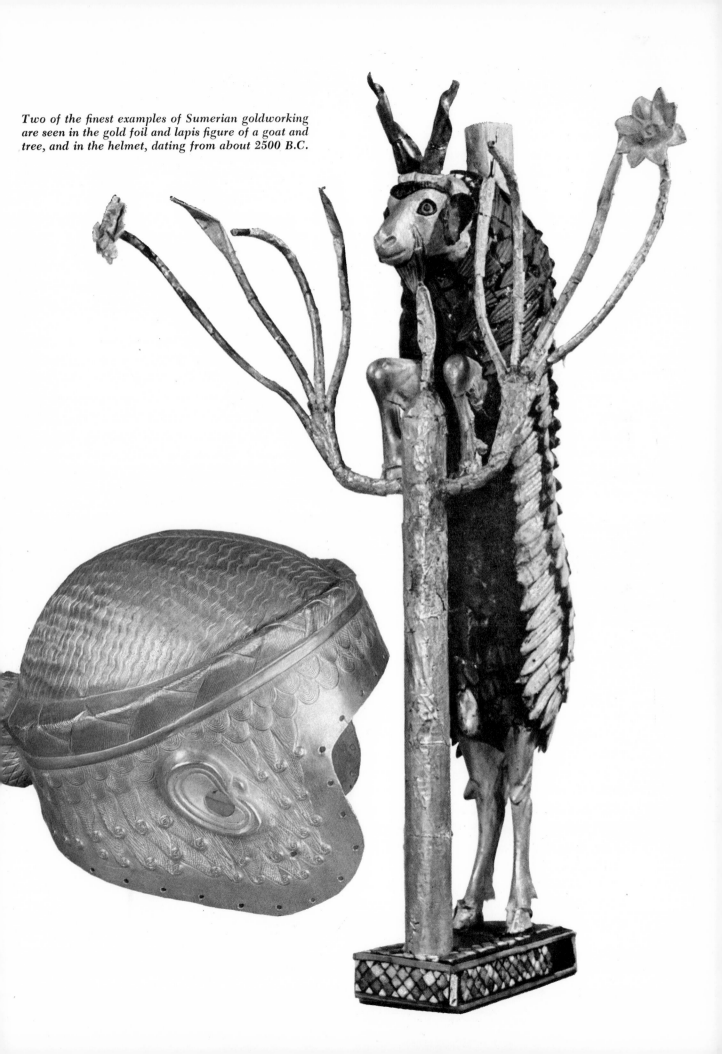

Two of the finest examples of Sumerian goldworking are seen in the gold foil and lapis figure of a goat and tree, and in the helmet, dating from about 2500 B.C.

foreign invasions and the city-states struggled among themselves for authority over neighboring areas. But although such conflicts were frequent they were rarely decisive. The various city-states continued to exist as separate contending entities, recognizing no single ruler or central authority.

The first ruler to bring the land of Sumer under one authority was Lugalzaggisi, king of Uruk. According to his own records, he extended the sway of the Sumerians from the Persian Gulf to the shores of the Mediterranean. His despotic reign was challenged and overthrown by the first great Semitic ruler of Mesopotamia, Sargon, a king whose exploits are abundantly documented on clay tablets that have survived from the period. In about 2300 B.C., Sargon founded his capital at Akkad, which was probably very near Babylon. A bronze sculptured head found at Nineveh and thought to be a portrait of Sargon, shows this great king as a handsome man with full sensuous lips, strong aquiline profile, luxuriantly curled hair, and noble beard. He was evidently a born general, too, capable of shrewd and far-ranging military maneuvers. He must also have had large armies at his command to achieve the total subjugation not only of Mesopotamia but also of its neighbors. Before he attacked the Sumerian city-states to the south, he was careful to protect his position by taking the northern towns of Mari, Assur, and Arbil. Then, in a short time, his armies overran the Sumerian cities and established him as "King of Sumer and Akkad," the greatest to bear that name.

Sargon was a statesman as well as a soldier, and he incorporated the Sumerian city-states into an Akkadian empire which lasted almost 150 years. His grandson Naram-sin pushed the frontiers of the empire to the mountains of Asia Minor, proudly boasting that he was "King of the Four Quarters of the World."

The Semites of Akkad had long traded with the Sumerians; they had adopted the Sumerian gods, and they had borrowed Sumerian script for writing their own language. Now, however, a new spirit finds expression in Mesopotamian culture. One has only to compare the lithe, fluid line of the sculptured soldiers of the Stele (or engraved pillar) of Naram-sin with the rigid figures on Eannatum's Stele of the Vultures (see page 53) to notice the change. Eannatum's Stele has great historical value, but Naram-sin's is a wonderful work of sculpture. With only fifteen figures, two formalized trees, a few upward-surging lines culminating in a conventional peak, the sculptor has depicted the successful attack by Naram-sin's armies on an enemy's mountain stronghold. The whole scene is alive with movement: the steady upward march of the Akkadian monarch's troops, an enemy falling back dying, another plunging from a rocky ledge, a third clasping his hands in entreaty, while towering over all stands the heroic figure of the king.

Semitic influence also shows itself in more realistic portrait sculpture and the vigorous treatment of animals, especially lions and bulls. Equally remarkable is the art of the engraver. The cylinder seals of this period writhe with life: Gilgamesh grapples with a buffalo, and on another seal, locks his powerful arms around a struggling lion, snapping its neck. There is an almost explosive quality in these tiny designs which foreshadows the terrifying violence of Assyrian art in later times.

There were further dynastic changes in Mesopotamia, of which only the broadest outlines concern us here. An invasion by eastern barbarians, the Guti from the Zagros Mountains, destroyed what was left of Sargon's Akkadian empire late in the third millenium. Once again there was disorganization in the land of Sumer.

The city of Lagash managed to escape the general chaos caused by the Guti, probably because of its military strength, and because it paid tribute to the invaders. Its governor, Gudea, beautified the city with temples and palaces, and with sculptures of such quality that they have become famous in our own day.

Urnammu, the founder of Ur's Third Dynasty, is depicted here, pouring a libation before a seated god who holds a measuring ring, line, and staff, the symbols of justice; below, the king carries construction tools for the building of the city's ziggurat.

MESOPOTAMIA

2. babylon and the age of hammurabi

THE great Babylonian king Hammurabi, who reigned from 1792 to 1750 B.C., is best known as one of the world's greatest—and earliest—lawgivers. While his was not the first legal code, it is one of the most important documents in human history. Much earlier codes, dating as far back as 2100 B.C. in the time of the Sumerian king Urnammu have survived, but Hammurabi's system of laws was much larger and more comprehensive, covering almost every kind of human activity.

There are laws concerning marriage and divorce (including a husband's responsibility for his wife's debts), property rights, liability for military service, sale of wine, deposits and debt, murder, assault, theft, and the responsibility of professional men to their clients. The death sentence was imposed for theft, adultery, and bearing false witness in cases that involved a defendant's life, and for false accusation. There were laws concerning inheritances, adoption, wages, slaves, agriculture and commerce.

Women were given special protection under the law, even though they didn't enjoy the same

This may be Hammurabi, the great ruler of Babylon, who is best remembered for the law code he established, one of the earliest legal systems ever devised.

A common theme in Mesopotamian art is that of man's struggle against wild beasts. In a detail of an Assyrian relief, opposite, the hero holds a lion cub. In the stone carving at right the hero tames a pair of lions. The figures below show a man, possibly the mythical hero Gilgamesh, grappling with two bulls.

social status as men. A woman could obtain a divorce if her husband neglected her, providing she could prove she had lived a blameless life. A concubine who had borne children to a man who sent her away was entitled to take her dowry with her, and the man was required to support her and his children by her.

The higher the social rank of the injured party, the harsher were the penalties for the crimes. Some penalties may seem excessive to us, but at least some have had later parallels in history. If, for instance, a doctor caused his patient to lose an eye, through carelessness or negligence, he lost one of his own eyes. Or if a builder constructed a house so carelessly that it fell on its owner, the builder was subject to death or at least a heavy fine. However, it does not appear from the court records of the time, that such harsh sentences were often imposed.

Such records as these help to give us a much more intimate picture of the Babylonian world than would be possible from the ruins of the cities and the chronicles of their kings alone. Another glimpse into the lives of ordinary men and women of the time is provided by the little cuneiform tablets upon which the folk wisdom of the people was summed up in their proverbs. Many of these axioms would seem immediately familiar to us, some 3700 years later.

*A restless woman in the house
Adds ache to pain.*

*Who has not supported a wife or child,
His nose has not borne a leash.*

*We are doomed to die; let us spend;
We shall live long, let us save.*

*You can have a lord, you can have a king;
But the man to fear is the [tax collector].*

This sculpture of a Sumerian scribe, a votive offering to his patron god, is similar in dress and physical characteristics to the figures on the Royal Standard of Ur.

Other Mesopotamian writings express the highest hopes of mankind. In the *Epic of Gilgamesh* is told the story of the first great tragic hero known to history. This superb dramatic poem was written at least 1500 years before the Homeric epics of the Iliad and the Odyssey. Miraculously surviving for thousands of years amid the rubble of vanished ancient cities, it was rediscovered by archaeologists within the last century. Its hero, the mighty Gilgamesh, was a legendary king of Uruk, which claimed to be the oldest of the Sumerian cities. Its theme is two-fold—man's conquest over his environment, and his yearning for immortality.

In the heroic figure of Gilgamesh are shown all the effort and striving, the terror and trials of the anonymous masses of the early Sume-

rian world. In one episode, Gilgamesh goes into the mountain forests with his good friend and companion Enkidu, to fell a cedar. They enter the dark woods and confront the god Humbaba, the frightful guardian of the forest and, according to modern interpretations, a symbol of evil.

For the clustering cedars
Made the way difficult and the going slow.
And as a first indication of their true intentions
In those parts, both Gilgamesh and Enkidu
Set their hands to the axes and attacked the trees . . .
Then the forest god Humbaba, struck back
And leaping up fully armed at the first onslaught
They fought back valiantly at the malignant anger
Unleashed upon them . . . And there was no pausing
For axes then, but swung swords began the sickling
Of all between them and that scourge . . . and the whirlwind
Scoured after them through agony of the cedar trees
Like a searching of bullwhips . . . and the thunderbolts
Bounced off the body-armor of those two heroes
A pattern of spent sparks off an anvil . . . And lightning crackled
About them balefully while they struck new knotted
Virulences of light out of the flame-forks
And cut them down . . . And there was just no harness
To put upon fighting bulls like those, as they drove on
Battering down, trampling, and crushing the indiscriminate
Heart out of that anger—forcing a final
Stranglehold of subjection upon their danger . . .

(This is a free translation, made by D. G. Bridson, an English scholar, in his book, *The Quest of Gilgamesh*).

Many of the tablets from which we have learned so much of Babylonian civilization date from the first half of the second millenium B.C. and are written in Sumerian cuneiform. The rest were found among the remains of the library built at Nineveh by Assurbanipal, the last great king to rule the Assyrian empire before it collapsed in the seventh century B.C.

The Elamites of southwestern Iran were, like other neighboring peoples, strongly influenced by Sumerian culture. The skill of the Elamite metalworkers is seen in this bronze axehead mounted with an electrum boarshead.

Among those archives was an account of the story of the Deluge, incorporated with the epic of Gilgamesh. This account came from sources written about 1500 years before the biblical story of Noah was set down, around 800 B.C. There is no evidence to suggest that any one great deluge actually did take place in Mesopotamia, but the valley was subject to local floods, and these may have been disastrous, within their limits.

Babylonian boys of good families were sent to school to learn to write the cuneiform system. They also learned the timeless myths surrounding the ancient gods, much as children today learn passages of our own great classics. Arithmetic was also taught, and students who aimed for higher government posts would go on to more complex mathematics such as algebra and geometry. It is interesting to note that their multiplication tables were based on a sexagesimal system—(a system based on units of 60) as we use the unit 10 in our decimal system. Our division of the hour into 60 minutes or 3600 seconds, and the circle into 360 degrees is an inheritance from the sexagesimal system of early Mesopotamian times.

The study of mathematics was important to the student who wanted to be a builder or surveyor, tax official or astronomer. If he wanted to become a physician, he would study anatomy and surgery, and learn an extensive catalogue of incantations and exorcisms for dealing with the demons who caused sickness. He would also learn the properties of many drugs, some of which are still used by doctors today. Over 500 such drugs are recorded on cuneiform tablets discovered at Nippur. Sumerian and Babylonian physicians understood the medicinal properties of myrtle, asafoetida, thyme and

This bronze head may be an Elamite monarch or priest.

Two human-headed bulls are conquered by a hero in this detail from the sound box of a harp (see page 50) found in the royal tombs at Ur.

cassia, and of such minerals as potassium nitrate and sodium chloride. They knew enough chemistry to make filtrates, and could also make a kind of soap.

Agriculture was also taught, and certain tablets give careful instructions about preparing the soil, plowing and planting, watering and harvesting.

If the student rose to high rank in the priesthood, he would have to give attention to learning rituals and spells, many of which seem like little more than black magic to us. However, each rite is described with careful precision, and it was essential that no detail be omitted, if the spell were to be effective, just as in modern science the least deviation from correct and controlled procedure can be disastrous. In the ancient world, magic was the only means believed to control the so-called supernatural forces, and its aims, at least, approximated those of modern science.

In one case, science did emerge from superstition. The Babylonians believed that the movements of the stars controlled the lives of men. The precise observations they made in following the movements of the stars and planets gave rise to the science of astronomy.

These ancient astronomers identified the major constellations, observed the five planets that are visible to the naked eye, and studied eclipses of the sun and moon, and even tried to predict them. They developed the zodiac as a map of the sky, the route along which the heavenly bodies traveled. The movements of the planets and the occurrences of the eclipses had, of course, magic significance to them: they regarded them as signs which foretold the destiny of battles and kings, crops and criminals. Using the zodiac, they cast horoscopes, with which they tried to determine which days were propitious and which were malign.

The Babylonians studied the heavens with awe and foreboding, for it was from the skies that most of the mysterious and powerful forces of nature emanated. Their god Marduk represented order, and the fertility of crops, and each year he was believed to battle anew with the goddess Tiamat, who represented the forces of chaos.

In celebration of this battle, there was an annual spring festival in Mesopotamia during which the priests recited the mythological accounts of Marduk, and the populace fought mock battles in the streets. During these religious festivals, the temple prostitutes plied their trade most assiduously. The public display of love was common in Babylon, and had none of the immoral connotations of later times. The "Town of the Sacred Courtesans" was Uruk, a city sacred to Ishtar, the goddess of love, beauty, and fertility, and also known as the courtesan of the gods.

The culture of Babylon was certainly sophisticated, and basically a culture of civilized men. But it was still rooted in the practices of those primitive ancestors of the Sumerians who moved down from their hills to settle in the marshy country along the banks of the Tigris and the Euphrates Rivers, from six to eight thousand years ago.

The triple-horned hat identifies this portrait as that of a divinity. The finely modeled head is Semitic in style and is about 3700 years old.

72

MESOPOTAMIA

3. assyria and

the kings of the world

AFTER the death of Hammurabi, the Babylonian world began a cultural and political decline. As it did so, a new Semitic people rose to power on the banks of the upper Tigris. These were the Assyrians, a ferocious people whose profession was war. In the Old Testament, accounts are given of their conquests and their persecutions of the nations which they laid waste. Then, in the nineteenth century, French and English archaeologists uncovered

the ruins of Assyrian cities and the modern world could see the palaces, temples and the images of the people for whom the Hebrew prophets had reserved some of their harshest denunciations.

The French archaeologist Paul Emile Botta and the Englishman, Austen Henry Layard, unearthed the ruins of the palaces of two of the greatest Assyrian cities—Nineveh and Calah, the latter now called Nimrud. Cuneiform inscriptions and magnificent carved reliefs revealed much of the political, military and religious aspects of Assyrian life. The reliefs showed one scene after another of warfare.

Winged bulls with human heads guarded the gates of Assyrian palaces. Their sculptors gave them five legs so that they would look realistic from the front or side.

Tall, bearded kings with cruel lips are shown standing in their war chariots watching the sack of an enemy city. Prisoners are being impaled on pointed spikes; an enemy ruler, staked out on the ground, is slowly being flayed alive by men with knives. Women and children are driven away captive; headless bodies float down the river. The fiercest denunciations of the Hebrew prophets do not damn the Assyrians as effectively as do some of their own pictures and inscriptions.

These savage scenes are executed with such ferocious strength, such violent yet disciplined force that they take the breath away. One can scarcely approach them without experiencing the same awe, almost terror, that they inspired at the time of their discovery.

To the Assyrians, life was war and their genius was concentrated upon it. Their armies were highly organized, and used iron weapons and such formidable engines as battering-rams and siege towers which, when pushed up to the walls of an enemy city, enabled them to pour down fire on their enemies while they themselves were protected by armor. Perhaps most frightful of all, however, was their calculated use of violence and terror.

Who were these people, capable of such violent and subtle cruelty, yet also of the execution of such beautiful works of art?

Some time between two and three thousand years before the birth of Christ, a stocky, Semitic people came from the west to settle on the upper banks of the Tigris in a region that is now northern Iraq. Assur, from which the name of these people is taken, was their chief city. These people were under Sumerian control for many centuries, but with the fall of the Third Dynasty of Ur in 2000 B.C., the Assyrians broke away from Sumerian control. In a land filled with ambitious rivals and beset by frequent foreign invasions, independence was precarious; in the eighteenth century B.C., Assyria became part of Hammurabi's empire, and was ruled from Babylon. Eventually it re-

gained its freedom but not until around 1200 B.C., with the collapse of the Hittite empire, was Assyria able to expand its borders.

During the next hundred years, several powerful kings held the throne. Tiglath-pileser I rebuilt the temples and palaces of the land, and restored its public works, and also became a military leader to be reckoned with by all contesting tribes and principalities. By 1100 B.C. the Assyrians had pushed their conquests west to the Mediterranean and north to Lake Van. But the next two hundred years saw a decline in Assyrian power, and Babylon, which it had conquered a century earlier, and the western territories were lost.

Then, in the ninth century B.C., Assurnasirpal II came to the throne, and Assyria began its march to power. An aggressive military genius, Assurnasirpal had inscribed on his records, "I, Assurnasirpal . . . the mighty king, king of the universe, the king without a rival . . . the mighty hero who treads on the neck of his foe . . ." And perhaps he was hardly exaggerating for he reorganized the Assyrian army and led it as far as the Phoenician coast, collecting tribute from the weaker cities and by-passing towns that might offer strong resist-

Fleeing from their Assyrian pursuers, refugees swim across a river using animal skins inflated with air as life preservers, in this Assyrian palace relief.

ance. Those that could not be ignored and did not immediately surrender were battered into submission and annexed to the Assyrian domain. Nimrud became the capital city, and the king restored this ancient city to its former grandeur.

Assurnasirpal's son, Shalmaneser III, continued his father's campaigns, waging furious wars against his neighbors. Twelve kings of Palestine and Syria formed an alliance against him, but in 854 B.C., he defeated them all, boasting that he had "scattered their corpses far and wide and covered the face of the desolate plain with their widespreading armies."

The nations conquered by the Assyrians lived restlessly under their despotic rule, and frequent rebellions broke out. But such revolts rarely met with success, and the subject nations were then punished with much harsher regulation. Less fortunate peoples were slaughtered or carried into exile. Many captives were enslaved and brought back to Assyria, where they labored to build the magnificent palaces,

and ziggurats, and the gigantic walls that made the Assyrian cities the wonders of their time.

The numbers of captives that must have been taken is enormous. Sargon II claimed that he led almost twenty-eight thousand inhabitants of Samaria as prisoners, and the annals of Tiglath-pileser III list town after town conquered in the district of Damascus; one provided eight hundred prisoners, another, seven hundred fifty, and a third, five hundred fifty. Year after year the Assyrians depopulated entire districts, erasing entire nations, and carrying off images of gods from their native lands.

Sargon's son Sennacherib made Nineveh his capital and he built a palace there adorned with gold, silver, copper, alabaster, ivory, and precious woods. In the extensive parks and gardens, mountain streams were diverted to provide water for exotic trees and flowers imported from other lands.

Yet this king who caused so many great works of art to be created was as ruthless and militant as his forefathers. When the city of Babylon rebelled against his rule, Sennacherib destroyed it: "The city and its houses, from its foundation to its top, I destroyed, I devastated, I burned with fire. The wall and outer wall, temples and gods, temple towers of brick and earth, as many as there were, I razed and dumped them into the Arahtu canal." It is no wonder that the Hebrews were terrified when Sennacherib's armies marched against Judah and besieged Jerusalem, where the King Hezekiah, in order to avoid the fate of Babylon, handed over all the silver from the temple and all the treasures of his own palace.

Egypt was next, and Sennacherib's son, Esarhaddon, took his armies a thousand miles overland to the Nile Delta and conquered Memphis, the ancient capital of the pharaohs. The Egyptians tried to expel their Assyrian masters but within a few years, the conquering armies had traveled up the Nile to Thebes and sacked it so thoroughly that it never recovered its ancient eminence.

In a number of ways, the Assyrians resembled the Romans of the Imperial Age. Perhaps a love of discipline and order gave them their formidable prowess in war and their efficiency as rulers. They were extremely capable engineers, devisers of ingenious military machines, and experts in siege warfare. Their armies were organized in regular formations according to arms—chariotry, cavalry, heavy infantry, light infantry and sappers. Such organization was not common before that time—even the mighty Persian armies of the fifth century B.C. were organized according to tribes and not according to the type of arms they carried.

In Assyria as in Egypt, much of the ruling class was related, by birth or marriage, to the royal family. Like most oriental despots, the Assyrian king had many children, not only by the queen but by the women of the royal harem, too. The king himself was both the chief priest and central figure in the religious cult, and as such, was the mediator between man and god. He was regarded as being totally sacred and lived an isolated existence, aloof from all ex-

78

cept his entourage of court officials, soldiers, and slaves, and the women of the harem.

Nevertheless, he was also never very far from the sights and sounds of the battlefield, for an Assyrian king shared fully with his soldiers in the hardships and dangers of a military campaign. One has the feeling that if an Assyrian monarch were unable to demonstrate his soldierly qualities, he probably would not have remained king for very long.

The subjects of the king could be divided roughly into three groups: the aristocracy, the

Assyrian wall reliefs show scenes of such ferocious yet finely controlled strength that they fairly take one's breath away. Above, King Assurpanipal is attacked by a wounded lion while beside the royal chariots another beast lies dying. Below, a wounded lioness drags itself along by its forelegs.

freemen, and the slaves. From the aristocracy came all the dignitaries—the governors, priests, court officials, and so on. The middle classes of freemen included not only bankers and scribes, but also many kinds of craftsmen. The freemen had to pay taxes, usually in the form of material goods or labor, and all fit males were liable for military service. In this middle group also were the merchants, who traded in slaves, horses, camels, and manufactured goods. Gold, silver, and copper were used as mediums of exchange, and by the eighth century B.C. coinage had come into use.

In late Assyrian times there was a large class of agricultural slaves attached to the land—if the land was sold, they were sold along with it. Most of the slaves, however, lived in the city and were engaged in domestic work. Some could own personal property, even land, and their lot, on the whole, appears to have been rather comfortable.

Small stone cylinders were used by many ancient peoples as personal signatures or seals.

During the reign of Assurbanipal, the last of the great Assyrian kings, the splendor of the empire reached its greatest height. During the years between 669 and 626 B.C., Assurbanipal enriched the palaces of Nineveh with precious metals and fine woods, and the parks and gardens with exotic flowers and trees. At the court and in the homes of the wealthy, there was a corresponding luxury and sophistication, as we can see from the depictions on stone reliefs.

Hundreds of sculptured scenes, carved on massive blocks of stone, are perhaps the most impressive legacy of the Assyrians. On many of them, the king appears as the awesome conqueror, with abject foreigners under his sword. Certain motifs appear over and over again—chariots and horses, bowmen in the midst of battle, cities besieged, captives being led into exile. The continual obsession with warfare, the Assyrian armies endlessly ravaging nation after nation, is ruthless almost to the point of monotony. There were other aspects to Assyrian art, however. The huge winged bulls that guarded the entrances to the palace represented some benevolent protective deity, and delicate ivory objects showed carved scenes of a more peaceful nature.

Only fourteen years after the reign of Assurbanipal, "the king of the world," the Assyrian empire collapsed. The reasons for this seemingly sudden disintegration are not entirely clear, but a number of causes were undoubtedly involved. Babylonia, along with other captive territories, had never ceased its resistance to Assyrian domination. Wars, and the suppression of rebellions drained Assyria's financial resources and took a great toll of its fighting men. The armies had to be filled by soldiers from Assyria's subject nations, whose loyalties were not, therefore, to be depended upon. After a three month siege by the combined forces of the Babylonians and the Medes, the Assyrian capital finally fell in 612, B.C. The country was divided between its two conquerors. The Medes took the region east and north of the Tigris River and the Babylonians, under their king Nebuchadnezzar, took the regions to the west and the south.

In the fifth century B.C., Herodotus, a man of the world, and not one to be easily impressed, visited Babylon and wrote a glowing account of what he had seen: "Babylon lies on a wide plain, a vast city in the form of a square, . . . with a circuit of some fifty-six miles, and in addition to its enormous size it surpasses in splendor any city of the known world. It is surrounded by a broad, deep moat full of water, and within the moat there is a wall fifty royal cubits (80 feet) wide and two hundred (340 feet) high. . . ."

While there are some discrepancies between Herodotus's account and the excavated remains of Babylon, his description is reliable enough in most respects.

The city contained three main districts, one containing one of the palaces of Nebuchadnezzar, another the temple of Marduk, adjoining the high ziggurat Etemenanki, the "tower of Babel." In the center of the city was the main palace of the king with its Hanging Gardens, the great Gate of Ishtar, and the famous Processional Way.

Nebuchadnezzar's main palace, built on a rise high above the city, must have been an overwhelming sight. In the throne room was a splendid wall relief of glazed bricks, representing a procession of yellow lions. Above them were garlands of colorful flowers and tall graceful columns shown against a background of blue tile.

In the northeast corner were the so-called Hanging Gardens, looking as if they were suspended between the earth and the sky. When the palace was discovered and excavated at the beginning of this century, the excavators found a large vaulted structure whose roof had over it a thick layer of earth. In one of the rooms under this earth roof was a strange three-shafted well which may have supplied water to the soil above, by means of a hydraulic machine. Thus the trees and lawns planted above may have been irrigated.

The word *hanging* is not a precise one, for its Latin original, *pensiles,* can mean either "hanging" or "in the form of a balcony." What made the Babylonian balconies one of the Seven Wonders of the World was the fact that they had extensive gardens laid out upon them.

A nation of merchants, the Babylonians derived much of their wealth from trade and commerce. The units of currency that occur so often in the Old Testament, the talent and the shekel, are Babylonian. Babylon's caravans moved along much-traveled routes to and from Iran, Syria, Palestine, and Asia Minor. Its ships sailed down the Euphrates and through the Persian Gulf to Telmun, to bring back the produce of Arabia and India.

Despite their wealth, however, the Babylonians were not able to control their empire for very long. Nabonidus, the last king of Babylon, who reigned from 555 to 538 B.C., was of Aramaean origin and chose to worship his native god, Sin, rather than the Babylonian Marduk. When the priests and the people turned against him, he withdrew to the town of Harran and left his son Belshazzar in charge of the capital. It was while Belshazzar was ruling in Babylon that Cyrus the Persian succeeded in taking the city. Despite the protection of its enormous walls, despite the fact that the citizens had provisions and water to withstand a long siege, Babylon fell. The Persian king, Herodotus reports, dug a canal that drained off the Euphrates river into a marsh, and his troops were then able to wade across the moat and into the city.

At the time of the Persian invasion there was a festival going on, and the prophet Daniel, an unwilling guest at the dinner, wrote: "Belshazzar the king made a great feast to a thousand of his lords, and drank wine before the thousand." While Belshazzar drank, Cyrus' men waded through the shallow river and burst in upon the unsuspecting city.

"In the same hour came forth fingers of a man's hand, and wrote . . . upon the plaster of the wall of the king's palace: and the king saw the part of the hand that wrote . . . *Mene, mene, tekel, upharsin* . . . thou art weighed in the balances, and art found wanting. Thy kingdom is divided, and given to the Medes and the Persians."

So Babylon fell to the Persians, who did not destroy it, as Sennacherib had done, but preserved the city as part of their Achaemenian Empire. Later it rebelled and was retaken by Darius. Even then, though its defenses were thrown down, the Persians spared Babylon, so that Herodotus, when he went there in the next century, could still see much to admire.

Today Babylon and the other once-great cities of Mesopotamia are little more than desolate, dun-colored mounds of dried mud, surrounded for the most part by desert or scrubby little fields. Yet the world their people created lives on. Every time we look at a watch or a compass, or use a protractor, we are thinking like the Babylonians, in multiples of sixty. When we study star maps or, at a less scientific level, read a column on astrology in a popular newspaper, we share something with the Sumerian and Akkadian priests who watched the cloudless heavens from their temple roofs. The more we learn of the world of the Sumerians and their cultural descendants in Babylon and Assyria the more we understand our debt, spiritual and material, to the civilization that first flourished in the Land Between the Rivers.

The ruins of the West Gate can still be seen at Babylon (right). *Below, the Ishtar Gate was decorated with tile reliefs of bulls and the dragon of Marduk.*

A Contemporary View
of the Land
Between the Rivers

AROUND THE YEAR 450 B.C., HERODOTUS,
THE GREEK HISTORIAN, WROTE AN ACCOUNT
OF THE MARVELOUS FERTILITY OF THE
MESOPOTAMIAN LANDS, OF THE BABYLONIAN
TEMPLE TOWERS, AND OF SOME OF THE
REMARKABLE SOCIAL CUSTOMS OF THE
NEAR EASTERN PEOPLE:

THE FERTILITY OF THE LAND. "The rainfall of Assyria is slight. . . artificial irrigation is used by laborers working hand-pumps. Like Egypt, the whole country is intersected by dikes; the largest of them has to be crossed in boats and runs in a southeasterly direction from the Euphrates until it joins another river, the Tigris, on which Nineveh was built. As a grain-bearing country Assyria is the richest in the world . . . so great is the fertility of the grain fields that they normally produce crops of two hundredfold, and in an exceptional year as much as three hundredfold. The blades of wheat and barley are at least three inches wide. As for millet and sesame, I will not say to what an astonishing size they grow, though I know well enough; but I also know that people who have not been to Babylonia have refused to believe even what I have already said about its fertility.

THE RIVER BOATS. "The boats which ply down the Euphrates to the city . . . are circular in shape and made of hide; . . . they are not fined-off or tapered in any way at bow or stern, but quite round like a shield. The men fill them with straw, put the cargo on board . . . and let the current take them downstream . . . Every boat carries a live donkey, . . . and when they reach Babylon and the cargoes have been offered for sale, the boats are broken up, the frames and straw disposed of, and the hides loaded on the donkeys backs for the return journey. . . . It is quite impossible to paddle the boats upstream because of the strength of the current, and that is why they are constructed of hide instead of wood.

This ivory handle of a fly whisk shows two figures kneeling by a sacred tree.

THE ZIGGURAT AT BABYLON. "The temple is a square building, two furlongs each way, with bronze gates, . . . it has a solid central tower, with a second erected on top of it and then a third, and so on up to eight. All eight towers can be climbed by a spiral way running around the outside. . . . On the summit of the topmost tower stands a great temple with a fine large couch in it, richly covered, and a golden table beside it.

BABYLONIAN CUSTOMS. "The dress of the Babylonians consists of a linen tunic reaching to the feet with a woolen one over it, and a short white cloak on top; they have their own fashion in shoes, which resemble the slippers one sees in Boeotia. They grow their hair long, wear turbans, and perfume themselves all over; everyone owns a seal and a walking stick specially made for him, with a device carved on the top of it, an apple, or rose or lily or eagle or something of the sort. . . .

In every village once a year all the girls of marriageable age used to be collected together in one place, while the men stood round them in a circle; an auctioneer then called each one in turn to stand up and offered her for sale, beginning with the best looking and going on to the second best as soon as the first had been sold for a good price. Marriage was the object of the transaction. The rich men who wanted wives bid against each other for the prettiest girls, while the humbler folk, who had no use for good looks in a wife, were actually paid to take the ugly ones, for when the auctioneer had got through all the pretty girls he would call upon the plainest or even perhaps a crippled one, to stand up, and then ask who was willing to take the least money to marry her—and she was knocked down to whoever accepted the smallest sum. The money came from the sale of the beauties, who in this way provided dowries for their ugly or misshapen sisters.

Next in ingenuity to the old marriage custom is their treatment of disease. They have no doctors, but bring their invalids out into the street, where anyone who comes along offers the sufferer advice on his complaint, either from personal experience or observation of a similar complaint in others."

The ivory carving below may represent Ishtar, the goddess of love, or one of her sacred harlots.

The ivory cheekpiece of a horse's bridle is Egyptian in style and shows a sphinx with a sacred sun disk upon its head.

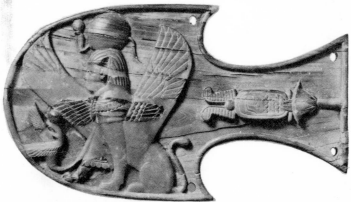

85

THE STRANGE WORLD OF THE INDUS VALLEY

ABOUT forty-five hundred years ago in the land now called Pakistan, there arose a nation of people who came down from their mountain homelands in the foothills of the Himalayas into the dangerous and inhospitable valley of the Great Indus River. This nation, often called the Harappa civilization, is one of the most recently discovered cultures of the ancient world; only in 1921, when an Indian archaeologist unearthed the buried remains of the great city of

One of the rare stone sculptures of the Indus Valley, this stern-faced man may be a deity or a priest-king.

Harappa, did it become evident that, as in Egypt and Mesopotamia, here was another river culture of the ancient world.

Part of the fascination of this Indian civilization is that it appears to have foreshadowed some features of the modern totalitarian state. Although the evidence is not conclusive, the the platforms on which rows of workmen pounded grain all suggest a strong state control.

Much about this civilization still remains to be discovered. There are substantial ruins of two great cities—Harappa and Mohenjo-daro—and many smaller sites spread over an im-

mense area that is more than twice the size of Egypt or Mesopotamia. But in this whole vast region, not one royal tomb has been discovered. The Indus Valley people had a writing system, but we cannot as yet read it. We know as little about their social customs as we do about their origins, or the reason for the collapse of their civilization. As for this last, there may be clues in the *Rig-Veda,* a collection of Hindu religious hymns that may prove to have a historical basis, like the *Iliad* and *Odyssey*.

The *Rig-Veda* is a saga of the Aryans, Indo-European invaders who swept down from the northwestern hills to the Punjab region around 1500 B.C. Eventually they settled throughout India. Their greatest god was Indra, from whom the country takes its name.

For a long time it was thought that these Aryans brought civilization to a barbarous land. However, one of Indra's names was *puramdara,* meaning "fort destroyer," and in the Rig-Veda, the god is described as destroying "ninety forts." Throughout the saga, there are many references to forts built of stone or mud brick.

Before the excavation of Harappa in 1921, there was no known building in all of India that could be dated earlier than 500 B.C. But now archaeologists began to read the *Rig-Veda* in a new light. The Indus Valley, it now appeared, had been the seat of a major civilization for a thousand years before the Aryan invasion. The forts that were destroyed by Indra and his people may well have been Harappa, Mohenjodaro, and the other Indian cities of the Indus Valley.

Archaeologists had long been intrigued by the huge mud brick mound at Harappa. It was difficult to excavate, however, since it was partly overlaid by the modern village. Also, in the nineteenth century, the mound had been heavily plundered by the builders of the Lahore-Multan railway, who used its material for ballast. However, the excavators were able to establish that it had once been a city of about three miles in circumference.

The first excavations, under the direction of a young Indian archaeologist, Rai Bahadur Daya Ram Sahni, brought to light a number of tiny seal stones bearing animal designs of great beauty, together with what was, apparently, some form of picture writing that bore no resemblance to any known script.

Precise dating of the mound was not possible, but from tools and other objects found deep inside, it was clear that the builders of the city had lived before the coming of the Aryans. The earliest level of culture has since been dated at about 2500 B.C.

Certain features of the ancient city were unique and have no parallel outside of India. Most remarkable was a great citadel rising high above the city and surrounded by a 45-foot wide baked-brick wall. North of the citadel was a group of barracks-like buildings and another group of huge granaries. Nearby were circular brick work platforms, each with a central hole in which had stood a heavy wooden

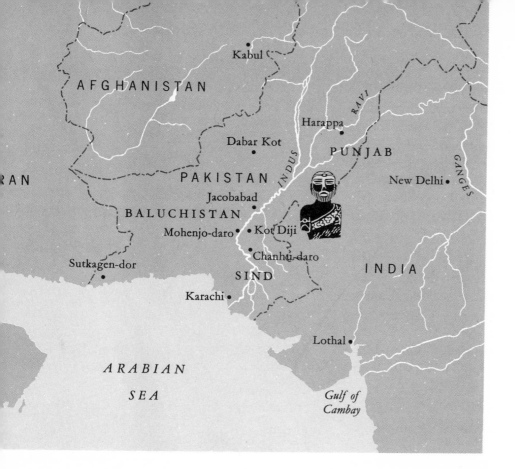

AFGHANISTAN

Kabul

Harappa

Dabar Kot

PUNJAB

RAVI

INDUS

PAKISTAN

New Delhi

GANGES

Jacobabad

BALUCHISTAN

Mohenjo-daro • Kot Diji

Chanhu-daro

Sutkagen-dor

SIND

INDIA

Karachi

Lothal

ARABIAN
SEA

Gulf of
Cambay

mortar. Indications were that these had been used for pounding grain, much as they are in present-day Kashmir. It would seem that the work was done under the supervision of the watchers in the citadel. The vast size of the whole complex and the apparent systematic planning strongly suggest that these were state granaries.

When the mound at Mohenjo-daro, 400 miles to the southwest, was excavated, it gave further strong evidence of a rigidly organized civilization. For here, uncovered after 3500 years, lay the skeleton of a vast city that had once swarmed with ant-like activity. Apart from the citadel, a great bath, and a granary, there is little evidence of monumental architecture. Instead, hundreds of small buildings, many of uniform size and construction, were laid out on a gridiron plan. The houses, with their windowless outer walls, fronted on narrow lanes that appear to have been deliberately zig-zagged, to break the force of the winds.

Like the Egyptians and the Mesopotamians, the Indus Valley people were dependent upon a powerful river in whose valley they had settled.

The round tower below was once a sunken well. Excavators left it standing when they dug through earlier layers to find the first level at Mohenjo-daro.

Some of the houses were planned with a feeling for spaciousness and dignity. A typical example has a porter's lodge at the entrance, and a passage leading to a pleasant courtyard that opens onto several rooms. Most of these buildings were of baked brick faced with plaster, and may have had an upper story approached by stairways that still survive. They contained bathrooms and latrines, often on two floors. Everywhere is clear evidence of controlled urban planning; earthenware drains encased in brick—one of the distinguishing marks of the Indus Valley civilization—carried away the sewage from the houses.

There were many shops, including one that contained sockets in the floor, possibly for wine jars, and that may have been a restaurant; numerous wells, both public and private, and small sentry boxes that that may have been for police or watchmen.

Mohenjo-daro also had its towering citadel and state granary. Within the citadel was a huge bath or tank, made watertight with mortar, bitumen, and four layers of brick. The emphasis on bathing, probably for purposes of purification, brings to mind current Hindu religious ritual; this and other evidence suggest that certain features of the Indus Valley civilization did indeed survive the Aryan invasion.

The Indus Valley culture seems to have arisen entirely on its own, owing nothing to Egypt, and little directly to Mesopotamia. However, seals with Sumerian markings, some ornaments and tools prove that there was at least some trade with the people who lived between the Tigris and Euphrates rivers.

Where did the founders of the Indus Valley civilization come from? We have already seen how some of the people who founded Sumer came from the western mountain valleys of Iran. It now seems likely that there were other agricultural communities on the eastern slopes of the Iranian mountains, and that it was among these groups that the earliest Indus Valley settlers originated.

The most important thing that these mountain people brought with them to the valley was not, perhaps, their bronze tools or weapons, but the concept of a civilized society. Such a society, whose people had the knowledge of writing and led an organized life centered in cities, had already developed in Mesopotamia. It may well have been that the hill people were aware of these developments beyond the Iranian plateau in Mesopotamia and had profited from this knowledge.

For centuries they had lived a closed, precarious and difficult existence in their mountain homes. But not far away lay the broad, fertile plains of the Indus and its tributaries, a dangerous land of deep jungle and wild animals. The land, perpetually fertilized by river-borne mud, was rich. There was an abundance of game and fish. And the river itself provided a natural highway linking and uniting a vast area. At some time, the people from the hills began to move down onto the plain. Diseases surely took a heavy toll. There were wild animals against which the only weapons were the bow and the spear, and the later settlers had to contend with hostile peoples as well. The mighty river, when in flood, was like a god in anger, fierce and uncontrollable, sweeping away farms, fields, men, and beasts. Yet the immigrants stayed on and fought. Thousands died, but others arrived to take their places. Gradually they learned to control the untamed elements of their environment enough to make city life possible.

Within not more than a thousand years these people had created their own civilization which depended on irrigation, flood control, and communal farming on a large scale. They built at least two big cities, traded extensively with other cultures, and developed a system of pictographs which were engraved on seals. And yet before the end of those ten centuries their civilization had begun to decline, and in 1500 B.C. it was overwhelmed and eventually disappeared almost without trace.

The little bronze dancing figure may be a Baluchi woman, identifiable by her bracelets and hairdo.

Indus Valley writing is shown on many of the seals of the country. The script can easily be seen above the bull on a little one-inch seal impression, enlarged here.

We have only the vaguest clues to the type of society that was created by these people. We know practically nothing of their religion, although the presence of numerous female figurines—possibly fertility goddesses—suggests that the earliest deities were female. And since in other centers of civilization the intellectual leaders were the priests, it is reasonable to assume that a similar situation would have existed in the Indus Valley. Yet so far, no temples have been positively identified, though on the seals, and among the statues unearthed in the two main cities, are figures that may represent gods.

There are also small clay statuettes representing female figures, nude except for necklaces and large headdresses. Some of these have smoke-stained little cups, suggesting that they may have been used for burning incense. Some of the seals are similar to the Sumerian ones, for example, a horned tiger being attacked by a bull-man recalls various Sumerian representations of battles between minotaurs and various other composite animals.

The inhabitants of the Indus were a great trading people. They imported not only Sumerian products but gold from southern India, silver, copper, and lapis lazuli from Afghanistan, and turquoise from Iran. In return, they may have exported copper, stone, ivory, wood, and certain animals. Among their agricultural products were wheat, barley, melons, peas, sesame, and possibly dates. They domesticated humped cattle, buffaloes, and perhaps horses, asses, cats, pigs, and camels. They also grew cotton and exported it to Sumer; they are the earliest people known to have cultivated this plant.

The Harappans had a system of weights and measures, the latter ranging from very large to tiny units. The higher weights, along with measures of length, followed the decimal system, although a binary system was used for weights of lower denomination.

But the principal source of wealth in the Indus Valley was the land which, though richly fertile, had to be protected. The people learned how to build dikes and dams and to raise their cities on mounds out of reach of the floodwaters. It must have been a constant, bitter struggle involving the communal effort of many thousands.

The state granaries, huge and severely functional, drew their supplies from a wide area. At Mohenjo-daro, archaeologists found an unloading area into which grain wagons were evidently driven. Above this area was a platform onto which the sheaves of barley could be hauled by ropes, after which they would be stacked in the huge castle-like structure, whose steep, forbidding walls were clearly designed to resist attack.

What sort of life was lived by the inhabitants of Harappa and Mohenjo-daro during the millennium that their civilization lasted? The cities

Animals were the chief subjects portrayed by Indus Valley artists. Shown opposite is a seal impression of a tiger, portrayed with both respect and terror.

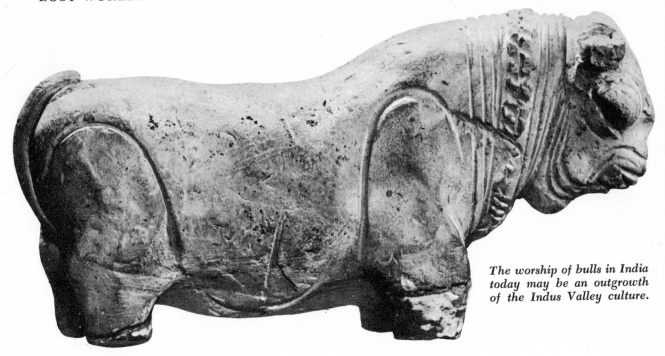

The worship of bulls in India today may be an outgrowth of the Indus Valley culture.

were planned with an eye to convenience, efficiency, cleanliness, and protection from the baking sun. The sanitary system and the numerous baths would have helped to keep down the plagues and epidemics that threaten large communities of people, especially in hot countries. Some of the buildings were large and comfortable, and even the smallest dwellings were probably no worse than the homes of millions of Indian and Pakistani artisans today. In the important respects of sanitation and water supply, they were superior.

No rich burial tombs have been discovered and such graves as have been found are evidently those of average citizens. There is nothing strikingly beautiful about the pottery, and such jewelry as has turned up is pleasing but unremarkable. Perhaps the most beautiful Indus artifacts are the tiny seals, about an inch in width. These are usually square, and each was carved in stone with a minute but delicately executed design, usually showing an animal. From these we know the types of wild beasts with which the Indus Valley folk were familiar.

They include the crocodile, rhinoceros, elephant, tiger, and antelope. Also a strange ox-like creature that appears to have only one horn. (Sir Mortimer Wheeler, perhaps the foremost scholar of the Indus Valley culture, has noted that according to both Aristotle and Ctesias, a Greek historian, the unicorn came from India.)

The seals were usually perforated for hanging around the neck or wrist and usually had short pictographic inscriptions. They were probably used, as were the Egyptian and Mesopotamian ones, for stamping the clay sealings that identified the ownership of certain goods.

Few examples of Indus statuary, either in stone or bronze, have been found, and those that do exist seldom portray the human figure. An exception is the slim, nubile figure of a dancing girl, her hand resting provocatively on her hip, and naked save for her numerous armlets. Of the small stone scuptures, perhaps the most striking is the steatite figure of a bearded man. It has a powerful but sinister face, narrow eyes, prognathous jaw, and receding forehead, the kind of face one can well imagine frowning down from the citadel on the ranks of laborers pounding grain on the work platforms. Numerous clay models of little animals have also been found, these executed with great finesse. Also there are many little toys, rattles, and terra-cotta dice.

As we have noted before, the most widely accepted theory about the disappearance of the Indus Valley civilization is that it was overthrown around 1500 B.C. by the Aryan invaders, under their war god, Indra. At Mohenjodaro, excavators came upon piles of skeletons of men, women, and children who had obviously been massacred and left to rot where they fell. All this pitiful human debris lay in the highest level of the city, the last one inhabited by the Indus-culture people. Lower layers of the excavations revealed that there must have been a period of progressive deterioration and decay before the final catastrophe wiped them out. At the lower levels were fine, well-made buildings of impressive size and construction. But higher up in the mound the buildings became shoddier and smaller. It seemed as if "squatters" had moved in, and the once dignified town mansions had deteriorated until they had become slum dwellings.

Such a decline in the civilization may have been caused by depletion of the soil, or a breakdown of the vast system of irrigation controls. Perhaps also the large forests that grew on the hills around the valley were depleted, by the use of vast amounts of wood for the baking of the mud bricks. Deforestation could well have increased the flooding of the Indus, just as it has altered the climate in other lands; the heavy rainfall, no longer partially absorbed by vegetation, could have stripped off the surface soil and swelled the already broad river to unmanageable proportions.

Compared with the richer and better known civilizations of Egypt and Sumer, the Indus Valley culture seems far less dramatic and splendid. Yet these people cleared the jungle, fought the wild beasts, tamed the flooding river, planned and built their cities, and created within a relatively short time a thriving civilization. We know little of who they were or where they came from, and nothing of their early struggles to achieve the mature culture at which we have discovered them. But we do know that they succeeded and that it was through their toil that a true civilization was born.

Many terra cotta toy figurines such as these have been discovered on archaeological sites in the Indus Valley.

CRETE

the island of minos

IT IS the usual role of scientists to dispel the romantic myths of earlier ages, substituting for them the cool, clear breath of logical explanations. Thus, ancient belief in the magic power of lodestone was cast away when it was explained that the magic was in fact, the force of magnetism, a quite reliable natural phenomenon with predictable characteristics. Thus also were legends about ancient and temperamental gods who controlled the winds and rain

Startlingly evocative of ancient legends are these stone bull's horns. Such horns were set on top of King Minos' palace at Knossos, to mark the spot as sacred.

and sun, discarded when the science of meteorology was born.

The scientific application of archaeology, however, has had a remarkably different effect: it has, within the last century, given credence to many of the ancient Greek legends related by Homer, Hesiod, and other poets whose works had for nearly 2,000 years been regarded as literary fantasies.

Nearly every school child knows the story of how Theseus, the Athenian prince, slew the Minotaur, the terrible beast, half man and half bull, that was kept in a labyrinth by Minos, the King of Crete. And nearly everyone, up until

97

Crete is the southernmost of a chain of islands that links Greece with the Turkish mainland. Mycenae, in Greece, and Troy, on the coast of Asia Minor, were also the sites of historic archaeological discoveries.

the last few decades, was introduced to such stories as charming Greek fairy tales. However, as we shall see, archaeological discoveries have proven not only that Homer's story of the Trojan War was based on historical fact, but also that even the legends of King Minos' labyrinth were based on real places and real people.

The modern archaeologist does not believe in the reality of the Minotaur, or in the existence of the ancient Greek gods, any more than

earlier scholars did. But it is no longer possible to think that these myths simply represent poetic or symbolic truths. The reality lies somewhere in between, for now the myths have been proven to contain elements of historical truth.

By 2800 B.C. two major civilizations had developed, one in Africa and the other in the Near East. Egypt was already trading commercially with the coastal cities of Lebanon and Palestine, and within a century or two, had also established trading contacts with the Aegean islands. A glance at the map will show that a chain of islands links Greece with the Turkish mainland; the southernmost and largest of these is the long, narrow, mountainous island of Crete.

During the nineteenth century, archaeologists had devoted most of their attention to the Greek mainland, not to the islands of the Aegean. Between 1870 and 1884, the brilliant and eccentric German amateur archaeologist, Heinrich Schliemann, had excavated at Troy near the Hellespont, and Mycenae, Tiryns, and Orchomenos in Greece. Schliemann believed, contrary to scholars and professional archaeologists of the time, that the Trojan War was an actual historical event. And he proceeded to confound the world by discovering the remains of buildings and arms, ornaments and other works of bronze, gold, and ivory, some of which closely resembled objects described by Homer in the *Iliad* and the *Odyssey*. These discoveries were of a type not previously seen in Europe. The art was exquisite—sensitive, vigorous, and disciplined. At the time that they were discovered, precise archaeological dating did not exist. In his enthusiasm, Schliemann attributed all of the objects to the period of the Trojan War, which was then thought to have occurred about 1190 B.C.

But other scholars were not so easily persuaded as Schliemann was, and a long and bitter controversy followed the Trojan discoveries. The Englishman, Arthur Evans, believed that the goldwork was older than the period of the Trojan War. Evans was fascinated with the Mycenaean treasure and after meeting Schliemann, spent much time examining the artifacts. A remarkable and complex man, Evans was extremely well-read in many fields, especially ancient history and prehistory. He also had almost microscopic eyesight when viewing things at close range and he studied the tiny markings on some of the smaller objects and wondered if they might be pictographs, in a hitherto unknown language. A vigorous man of action as well as a highly respected scholar, he made several trips to Greece and Sicily in pursuit of the answer to the question that most puzzled

The tapered columns of the portico of the palace of Minos at Knossos were smaller at the base than at the top. They probably were derived from the tree trunks which had once been used to support buildings, and which were placed upside down so that they would not take root and grow again.

These are the remains of the queen's apartments in the Knossos palace. Rectangular rooms and assymetrical plans were typical of the architecture of the Cretans.

him, which was, whether prehistoric Greece had had a writing system that had since been lost.

One day he came across some tiny bead seals in an antique dealer's shop in Athens. Examining them, he noticed some tiny marks that he again thought might be writing symbols. Upon questioning the dealer, Evans found that the seals had come from Crete. There, they were called *galopetres,* or "milk stones" because the peasant women wore them as charms when they nursed their children.

Soon after, Evans sailed to Crete, and immediately fell in love with the island, with the snow-capped Mount Ida, where Zeus himself was born. On Crete Evans found not only "milk stones," but potsherds, gems, and the remains of prehistoric settlements. Homer had written of Crete's lovely landscape and its ninety cities, one of which was Knossos where

100

"King Minos ruled and enjoyed the friendship of almighty Zeus."

Knossos still existed, although it was a small village now. There was, however, a large mound there, and excavations had already been begun by another archaeologist, who had found remains of massive walls and storage jars.

Still hoping to find clues to a writing system, Evans decided to dig at the mound which, if it proved to be another Mycenaean palace, might contain such archives as had been discovered

The terra cotta tub below *was about the size of a Victorian hip bath. The vase shown next to it was made of steatite and is known as the Chieftain's Cup.*

at Assurbanipal's palace at Ninevah. After somewhat lengthy political negotiations, Evans obtained permission to begin digging, in March of 1900. And almost at once, he came upon a great labyrinth of buildings. He soon found the palace storerooms, with great stores of jars that had once contained olive oil, wine, honey, figs, and other products of the island. And then he came upon what he had been looking for—the first hoard of clay tablets, inscribed with symbols, not Egyptian hieroglyphs, not Sumerian cuneiform, but a script he had seen on another tablet, one had come from Knossos.

Evans was subsequently proved correct in his belief that the civilization that had flourished in Crete was extremely ancient. When more precise scientific dating became possible, it was shown that the treasures found by Schliemann at Mycenae did not date earlier than 1600 B.C. At Knossos, however, Evans was able to trace the development of a civilization from 3000 B.C. down to about 1150 B.C.

Evans devoted thirty years and a considerable part of his personal fortune to the excavation and restoration of the Knossian palace. While he never succeeded in deciphering the inscriptions on the clay tablets, his interest in the Minoan writing system remained undiminished. His monumental work of scholarship, *The Palace of Minos,* is, with the restored palace, a memorial both to his genius and to his firmly held beliefs.

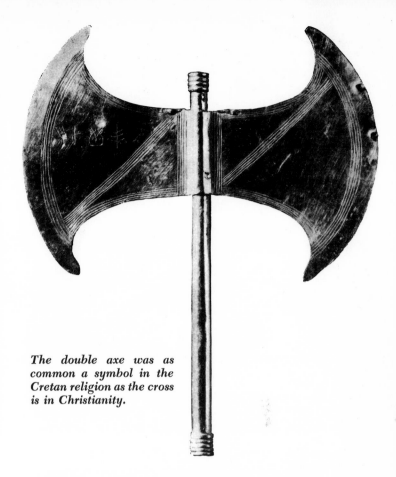

The double axe was as common a symbol in the Cretan religion as the cross is in Christianity.

Numerous other scholars have also helped to unravel the mystery, and not all have agreed with Evans. Later interpretations have caused earlier opinions to be revised.

However, Evans' first discoveries at Knossos astonished the archaeological world. He showed that the palace, built around a large central courtyard, was indeed truly labyrinthine in its complexity. About the central court was a maze of halls, private chambers, storerooms, stairs, ramps, and other areas. On one of the plastered interior walls was the painted fresco of a Minoan man, the first such representation to be discovered. It recalled to Evans a tomb painting found at Thebes in Egypt, which showed the reception of certain visiting foreigners. They were non-Egyptian in both physique and dress: thin-waisted, elegant, with

OVERLEAF: *A fresco from the palace at Knossos illustrates the Minoan sport of bull-leaping. At left, a dancer prepares to somersault over the bull, as the youth before her has done. The third acrobat stands poised to catch and steady the first two as they land.*

101

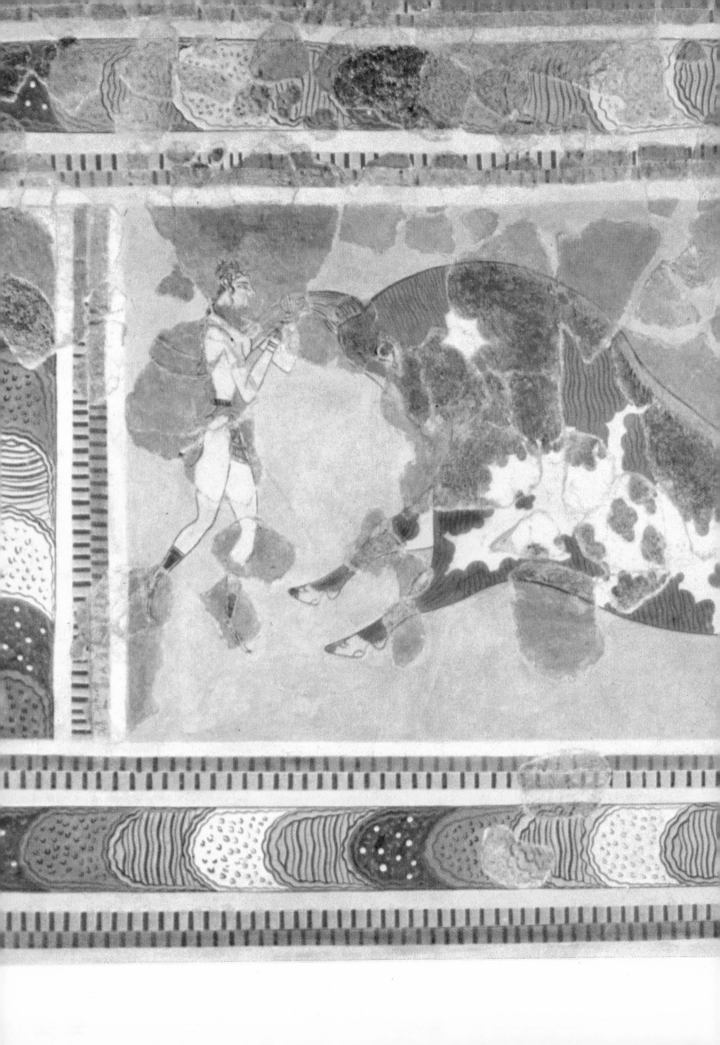

their dark curled hair worn in a side lock falling over one shoulder, and attired in short kilts. Similar figures appear in other wall paintings. Sometimes the gifts they carried to present to the Egyptians resembled objects found by Schliemann at Mycenae. The figure shown in the fresco uncovered by Evans' workmen was of just this kind. Here, then, was one of the mysterious *Keftiu,* as the visiting foreigners were called in the Egyptian painting, who traded in the Nile Valley city in the fifteenth century B.C.

To one side of the Central Court in the palace at Knossos was the Throne Room, in which stood a thirty-four-hundred-year-old alabaster

The bull's head at left is a rhyton, or drinking horn. Below, an audience of courtiers and ladies watches a ceremonial dance or performance of bull-leaping.

throne, the oldest one in all of Europe. In many of the other rooms there were marks of fire, indicating that the palace had been destroyed in flames.

On the side of the palace that faced the sea, the excavators found a monumental gateway. This, too, had been magnificent in its time, but what was most remarkable was the painted fragments of a plaster relief of a charging bull.

By this time Evans and his co-workers had begun to share Schliemann's respect for the ancient myths. There was the bull's head rhyton or stone jar, found at Mycenae; one could not help but be reminded of the legend of Europa who had been carried to Crete by Zeus, disguised as a white bull. One encountered the animal again and again.

Soon the archaeologists discovered other frescos which brought them closer and closer to the myth of Theseus and the Minotaur. One of these depicts another charging bull, but this time it is shown with human figures. One girl appears to be grasping one of the bull's horns. Another girl, standing behind the animal, is poised on the balls of her feet, her arms outthrust. And in the center of the picture, a male athlete is in the act of somersaulting over the bull's back, (see pages 102-103).

The seven youths and seven maidens sent from Athens to be sacrificed to the bull monster within the labyrinth—was this, after all, merely a fantastic legend? One may imagine the discussions and arguments that went on between Evans and his colleagues. The feat depicted in the fresco seemed impossibly dangerous and difficult, yet it was done. Another fresco shows a number of men and women in a grandstand, watching some kind of public performance. They are evidently members of the court, very fashionably dressed and coiffeured, although their bodices are so décolleté that their breasts are entirely bared. What event are they watching or waiting for? Perhaps it is the performance depicted in the other fresco, and perhaps this was part of a religious ceremony or ritual. In the center of the audience scene is what appears to be a shrine with tapering pillars representing the horns of a bull.

Two seals depict tumblers performing handstands and a bull-leaper beginning his somersault over a bull.

For what deity was this shrine intended? As in other eastern religions, the principal Minoan deity is always a goddess. (It was Cretans of later times who boasted that their island was the birthplace of Zeus.) Although male deities were shown in lesser positions, the goddess reigns eternally. She is shown again and again in slim-waisted figurines with belled or flounced ankle-length skirts. Sometimes her arms and upper back are covered. She also appears frequently on Minoan or Mycenaean seals or rings, sometimes with other figures, sometimes in a sacred grove. In some, she appears to be wearing puffed sleeves, but always the breasts are bare, and in some, the goddess is naked to the waist.

In the Central Sanctuary of the palace at Knossos the excavators found an exquisite statuette in faïence, of the Minoan goddess. In each outstretched hand she holds a writhing snake. Among primitive peoples, even today, the snake is frequently associated with the earth, and earth worship. For that reason, this figure is called either the snake goddess or the earth goddess.

In ancient religions in which sexual or fertility symbols play a large role, the figure of the earth mother is almost universal. In Neolithic times, she appeared as a pregnant woman. In the Near East she appeared as Diana of Ephesus or as Ishtar; in Minoan Crete she was sophisticated, even elegant. The whole palace of Minos was dedicated to her. In classical Greece she survived as Demeter, the goddess who increased the fertility of the fields; Aphrodite, the goddess of love, Athena, the warrior, and Artemis, who had power over the wild beasts were all aspects of this earth mother figure.

Little by little, with infinite care and patience, Evans and his colleagues restored the crumbling palace, the magnificent Great Staircase, and the rooms to which it led. The result is awe-inspiring. When one descends the staircase or stands in the dimly-lit frescoed rooms of state, one feels close to those remote people who were so extremely religious, yet so full of a childlike *joie de vivre*.

Another sacred symbol that frequently appears in Minoan ruins is the *labrys,* or double axe. Evans and others have suggested that it was associated with some rites to propitiate infernal powers. One of the palace rooms whose walls are decorated with such symbols, is called the Hall of the Double Axes. On the walls of another room, Evans found pictures of the huge leather, figure-eight-shaped shields which are so often encountered in Minoan and Mycenaean art. Other rooms appeared to be the queen's chambers, and nearby, a room contained a small earthenware bath. Also near was a small chamber containing what was a latrine. Each area of the palace was served by a drainage system that fed into the main channel, which, in turn, emptied into the river east of the hill. The Minoans apparently had highly advanced knowledge of hydraulic engineering 3500 years ago, as their methods of channeling water throughout the palace rooms show.

Other Minoan palaces and villas were built in a fashion similar to the great Knossian pal-

Not surprisingly, the Cretans were largely dependent upon the bounty of the sea. The octopus jar above is a reminder of the island's fishing industry.

ace. All had stone walls reinforced by timber, tapered wooden columns, light-wells, large halls, and bathrooms and toilets. Often, the walls were painted with frescos, and the symbolic double axe appeared on sacred pillars. At the main palace there were storage magazines, offices for clerks and administrators, and workshops for many craftsmen.

Of course there were houses for people other than the royal family, and ancient towns of more modest buildings have been found throughout the island.

Among the finest products of the Cretan workshops were the jars and vases in which the Minoans stored olive oil and wine. Craftsmen learned to make the famous "eggshell ware," exceptionally delicate shell-like vessels, and the painting of these vases became a fine art. The Minoan pottery that has survived is some of the most beautiful that has ever been made.

The Minoans were, naturally enough, a great seafaring people. Most of their wealth came from their extensive maritime trade, and there are many evidences of ancient ports throughout the island. To what extent they established colonies in other lands is uncertain, but many of their trading posts did become permanent settlements.

The great contemporary civilizations of Egypt, Mesopotamia, and the Indus Valley grew up along fertile river valleys. But Crete is a mountainous island with no large rivers and few plains. What, then, was it that favored the development of such a highly distinctive culture?

A number of factors probably contributed, the most important one being Crete's geographic position. It was too far from the shores of Africa or the Near East to be subject to invasion or foreign influence, and so could develop as an independent culture. Yet it was near enough to both continents to trade with them. Also, there were few dangerous wild animals on the island, surely an advantage to early settlers. In ancient times, it was probably far more fertile than it is today, and was richly forested with cedars, oak, fir, and cypress.

We don't know exactly when Greece was settled, but it seems likely that people from the east began to move in to both the mainland and to the islands between 5000 and 4000 B.C. In the centuries between 3000 and 2500 B.C., the Cretan peoples grew and prospered. Even then, they apparently were in touch with Egypt, whether by trade or by immigration. At any rate, Egyptian stone vases of Predynastic and Early Dynastic periods have been found on the island.

The Cretans made beautiful stoneware themselves, and also, reminiscent of Egypt, palettes for grinding eye paint; they also grew papyrus and sugar cane, in the Egyptian tradition.

These people built complex houses, farmed the land, and raised livestock. Apparently never threatened by foreign invasion, they did have to cope with certain natural disasters, however, for the island was beset by earthquakes.

By 2500 B.C., the Cretans had begun to make their implements out of copper, rather than stone. Egyptian influences may have been responsible for the change. At any rate, within the next few centuries, contacts between Egypt and Crete became much more frequent, and the influence of each country upon the other became increasingly evident, especially in the arts and crafts of each nation.

Although we often refer to the "Greek mainland," Greece and the Aegean islands were occupied by a non-Greek speaking people before 1900 B.C. Words that end in *ssos* (Knossos) or *inth* (as in labyrinth or Corinth) are not Greek. Such word endings do appear in the language of Anatolia, however, strongly suggesting that the pre-Greek peoples of the mainland and the islands spoke the same language as the Anatolians, to whom some of them may have been related.

A primitive form of writing, of simple pictographs, has been discovered on seal stones and clay tablets of the Early Bronze Age in Crete. This script later developed into what Sir Arthur Evans called Linear A, one of the two linear systems he recognized on the Knossian tablets.

By 2000 B.C. the island civilization was well established. At this time, the foundations for the great palaces at Knossos, Phaistos, and Mallia were laid. No royal residences had been erected prior to this time, and no one has satisfactorily explained why these three palaces should suddenly be built. We don't know who the first rulers were who occupied them, but one is reminded of the legend of Europa who, after being carried off by Zeus to his island home, bore the god three sons, Minos, Sarpedon, and Rhadamanthus.

In many places on the island, archaeologists have discovered sacred groves and caves and rock shelters, which were sanctuaries or cult centers for the popular religion. In the sanctuaries, many little clay figurines have been found. Some of these reveal the occupation of the donor . . . on one bowl is shown a shepherd and his flock, on others, many painted cattle are depicted. Most interesting are the statuettes of bulls with little human figures clinging to their horns. Perhaps the Knossian sport of bull-dancing shown in the palace frescoes began as a sport among the young herdsmen of the plains.

The chief deity appears to have been a goddess, queen of the animals, the sea, the mountains, or the infernal powers. Although she is depicted in many small statues and reliefs, the Cretans built no great temples to her or other deities, nor did they model any heroic sculptures of their gods. Unlike the Egyptians and Mesopotamians, the Minoans apparently were not unduly awed by the supernatural.

Minoan civilization reached its highest point between 1700 and 1400 B.C. When Evans and other excavators were digging around the palaces and great mansions, they were struck by the fact that these buildings apparently had needed rebuilding time after time. It has been suggested, by Evans and others, that since Crete has been subject to earthquakes at fairly regular intervals during the past 700 years, earthquakes were also frequent in ancient times. According to Evans, the space of time between earthquakes, as known from more recent records, corresponded exactly with the intervals between the rebuilding of the Knossian palaces and villas. Also, in the ancient palaces there was evidence of sacrifice to the infernal powers (which were undoubtedly associated with the awesome rumblings of the earthquakes), before each rebuilding took place.

Poseidon, the Greek god of the sea, was also known as the "earth shaker," and Evans wrote, in recounting the occurrence of an earthquake in 1926, "the movement which recalled a ship in a storm, though only of a minute and a quarter's duration, already began to produce the same physical effect upon me as a rough sea. A dull sound rose from the ground like the muffled roar of an angry bull . . ." "It is something to have heard with one's own ears the bellowing of the bull beneath the earth, who, according to a primitive belief, tosses it with its horns . . . the constant need of protection between these petulant bursts of the infernal powers explains the Minoan tendency to concentrate their worship on . . . their great goddess . . . the Lady of the Underworld."

The last, most catastrophic destruction of Minoan structures is believed to have occurred around 1450 B.C. Was it an earthquake? Or perhaps the result of armed attack? The latter explanation is supported by the evidence of great and widespread burning of the many Minoan settlements at the same time. Also, the Mycenaeans on the mainland, a powerful and warlike people, became dominant in the Aegean only after the fall of Knossos.

Like the Etruscans, the Minoans suffer from having their history written by others. We are left only with their buildings and artifacts, and with the superb Cretan landscape which is still enough to excite our imagination.

A seal impression shows a chariot drawn by two goats and may represent a scene from a pageant, perhaps connected with some Minoan religious ceremony.

MYCENAE

home of gods and heroes

IN Greek mythology Thessaly, a region in the northern part of Greece, was supposed to be the birthplace of the gods. It was also the legendary scene of the creation and the flood; and Mount Olympus, the highest mountain in the area, was the home of the immortals. We don't know when the first men settled in Greece, but it is interesting that the earliest remains of human habitation in the land were found in Thessaly and in nearby Boetia.

The citadel at Mycenae overlooks broad and fertile plains. The grave circle shown here is on the lower part of the acropolis; below were houses and shops.

Archaeologists believe that the first settlers in Greece did not speak the Greek language. The Neolithic dwellings of these people indicate a strong tie with Troy, and other peoples of Asia Minor, whose early settlements were built in the same distinctive fashion.

Heinrich Schliemann's excavations at Mycenae, on the other hand, revealed a vigorous and well-marked Late Bronze Age culture of Greek-speaking people. This later civilization flowered suddenly around the turn of the sixteenth century B.C., and lasted for four hundred years or more. In its early stages, it showed strong influences from Crete, whose culture

111

had been flourishing for hundreds of years. Mycenae, however, became dominant in the Aegean area from about 1400 to 1200 B.C. Then, shortly after the Trojan War, it rapidly declined, leaving behind only the legends of its glory and the ruins of its impressive monuments.

At the beginning of the second millennium B.C., bronze was coming into use and high civilization was just beginning in Crete and on the mainland. Between 2000 and 1700 B.C., the first palaces were being built in Crete. On the mainland, waves of invasion and immigration were taking place. Many scholars believe that these settlers were the first Greek-speaking people to enter Greece. They may have come from somewhere in the north and founded a warrior aristocracy that is described in the Homeric epics. However, there is little actual evidence to support this theory and it seems more likely that, like the earlier settlers, they came from Anatolia. For one thing, the invaders brought with them a technique for making a pottery called Gray Minyan Ware, which was known only to one other people, the invaders of Troy and neighboring areas of western Anatolia, who settled in these regions at about the same time, in 1950 B.C.

Wherever the Mycenaeans came from, they were strongly influenced by the Minoan culture of Crete. Sir Arthur Evans firmly believed that the Cretans colonized not only the islands but also parts of the Greek mainland. And certainly, objects found in the Mycenaean shaft graves, which can be dated between 1600 and 1500 B.C., were surely made by Cretan craftsmen. Yet there was opposition to this point of view. Many archaeologists pointed out that there were major differences between the palaces of Crete and Mycenae, which indicated different cultural heritages. In Crete, the large central court was the most important architectural feature. At Mycenae, however, the distinctive thing was the *megaron,* a square hall that contained the king's throne and a large,

fixed circular hearth in the center. This hearth was surrounded by four pillars which supported the roof.

In the Palace of Nestor at Pylos, such a megaron still exists. It is very much like the building described by Homer in the *Iliad.* Nestor's daughter, Nausicaa, directs Odysseus to her father's palace, saying, "Directly you have passed through the courtyard and into the buildings, walk quickly through the great hall (megaron) until you reach my mother, who generally sits in the firelight by the hearth, weaving yarn stained sea-purple, and forming a delightful picture, with her chair against a pillar and her maids sitting behind. My father's throne is close to hers, and there he sits drinking his wine like a god."

At this time, such buildings of the Mycenaean plan did not exist in Crete. In the island palaces there were no permanent central hearths, and no principal porch, as on the mainland buildings.

Another major difference between Cretan and mainland structures is apparent in the two famous grave circles and their shaft graves, at Mycenae. Such graves were built seven hundred years earlier at Alaja Huyuk, in central Anatolia. The graves show, according to the archaeologist Sinclair Hood, "a striking mixture of the barbaric and the civilized." Some of the artifacts found in the graves, such as the amber beads that may have come from the Baltic show the influence of distant lands. The horse-drawn chariots that appear on the Mycenaean grave stelae were certainly not representations of anything Cretan; they came from Western Asia.

Even so, the influence of Minoan art was strong and enduring. It may be that the Cretan bronze- and gold-work was acquired by peaceful trading—or by looting Minoan settlements. The Mycenaeans could have persuaded Cretan craftsmen to work on the mainland, or they also could have carried them off as slaves and forced them to do so. Such practices are not unknown in later times, and it may have been so in prehistoric Greece. At any rate, it does not necessarily mean that Crete dominated and controlled the mainland.

In comparing Cretan and Mycenaean cultures, the question of these ancient worlds as described by Homer arises. The *Iliad* and the *Odyssey* were composed around 800 B.C., about four hundred years after the Trojan War took place. Both poems are a strange mixture of the society that Homer himself knew, and an archaic way of life resembling the one revealed by the excavations at Mycenae and similar sites. Homer describes bronze swords, chariots, and Hector's great oxhide shield which bumped against his neck and ankles as he walked. Such shields are depicted on inlaid daggers found in the shaft graves at Mycenae, although they were unknown in Homer's time.

The buildings and ivory-mounted furniture found in the graves are very much like those described by Homer, and his account of a golden cup decorated with doves is like one found in a shaft grave, as is his account of a great helmet adorned with slivers of boars' tusks.

In Homer's own time, warriors no longer fought in chariots; they used iron rather than bronze weapons, and they carried much smaller shields. The kings and rulers of Homer's period certainly did not possess the rich trappings and palaces described in the two great epic poems.

Homer drew his material from legends that had been passed down by word of mouth for many generations. The first of his poems, the *Iliad,* tells of the "wrath of Achilles," and describes the Trojan War. The *Odyssey* tells of the wanderings of Odysseus and of his return to his home in Ithaca. Other later Greek poets drew on the same legends, and the great Greek dramatists of the classical period, Aeschylus, Sophocles and Euripides, had access to the same material, telling us stories of the ancient heroes that Homer doesn't even mention. But all appear to be based to some extent on the Mycenaean civilization several centuries earlier.

The themes of these epics and dramas deal with events that both preceded and followed the Trojan War. From an archaeological point of view, they have a peculiar interest, for they abound in place names such as Mycenae, Thebes, Orchomenos, Tiryns, Pylos, Iolkos—all of which were the residences of Mycenaean (or Achaean, as Homer terms it) royalty. And when archaeologists began to dig at these places, the remains of Mycenaean settlements were revealed.

By the sixth century B.C. these cities had ceased to be important, although the classical Greeks of this later period believed the Homeric legends and knew many of the cities which had flourished some seven hundred years earlier.

This golden cup, found in the shaft graves at Mycenae, has handles decorated with birds like King Nestor's cup, described by Homer in the Iliad.

113

Homer wrote of "Tiryns of the great walls" and "Mycenae, rich in gold." The great walls of Tiryns are still there to be seen, and Schliemann found that Homer's description of Mycenae was confirmed by his excavations.

Long before Schliemann's time, Greek and Roman visitors had seen and described Mycenae. In the second century A.D., Pausanias, a Greek traveler, wrote that the walls were still preserved, "as well as the gates over which the lions stand." This gate, once the main entrance to the citadel, is still there today. Two great lions, posed facing each other, fill the pediment above the opening. Their heads have long since disappeared but the rest of the great composition remains as the oldest surviving example of monumental sculpture in Greece. And it is one of the most famous. Beneath these figures and through the portal, Agamemnon, the great king of Mycenae, led his armies at the start of their expedition to lay siege to Troy.

Great walls, called Cyclopean by later Greeks who could only conceive of their being built by that legendary race of giants, sur-

rounded the fortress. They still exist today, and in some places are more than thirty feet thick. At one point, near the Lion Gate, the walls surround the shaft graves excavated by Schliemann. Outside the walls are several magnificent tombs, built in the shape of a gigantic stone beehive. Called a tholos (or in the plural, tholoi), they were built later than the shaft graves although prior to the Trojan War.

The most famous of these great tombs is called the Treasury of Atreus (who was the father of Agamemnon). It is built of fitted stones which rise in a perfect cone shape. The massive lintel above the seventeen-foot doorway weighs more than 100 tons, a more enormous building stone than any used even in the great Egyptian pyramids. The interior walls were originally studded with bronze ornaments, and on the outside, sculptured columns of green stone flanked the entrance. Above this opening was a carved panel of various-colored stone. This three-thousand-year-old sepulcher is one of the architectural marvels of the ancient world.

114

A bronze dagger inlaid with silver and gold shows hunters attacking a lion. The Mycenaeans were profoundly impressed by the power of these animals and often depicted them in their art. The figure-eight shields and clothing of the hunters show the influence of the Minoans.

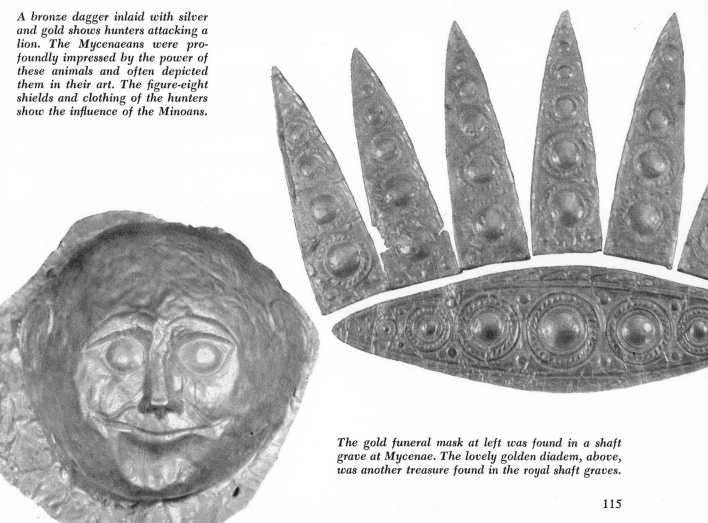

The gold funeral mask at left was found in a shaft grave at Mycenae. The lovely golden diadem, above, was another treasure found in the royal shaft graves.

The Mycenaean warrior, carved of ivory, wears a hel-met made of boar's tusks and carries a figure-eight shield, such as those described by Homer in the Iliad.

The mainland of Greece was not a unified realm but rather an assemblage of kingdoms. Although the rulers of each domain appeared to owe feudal allegiance to Agamemnon, king of Mycenae, they fought against as well as alongside each other.

The kingdom of Achilles was in Thessaly. The wrath of Achilles, described by Homer, was directed toward Agamemnon, because the Mycenaean king had claimed a slave girl whom Achilles had won in battle. Achilles' anger fed upon itself, supported by long-suppressed resentment of a strong and independent spirit against his distant overlord.

When Sir Arthur Evans was excavating the remains at Knossos on Crete, he discovered evidence of three writing systems. One was a form of hieroglyphics, and the others were the so-called Linear A and Linear B scripts. None, however, had been deciphered up to the time of Evans' death in 1941. Then, in 1952, a brilliant young English architect named Michael Ventris announced that he believed that he had "cracked" the Linear B script, and that it represented an early form of the Greek language. For the first time, it could be proved that the Mycenaeans were Greek, and now they would be allowed to speak for themselves. This was perhaps the greatest feat of decipherment ever achieved, for Ventris had no bilingual clues to guide him; that is, no one has yet found identical texts written in both Linear B and in a previously known script.

It took Ventris sixteen years to decipher the script. He had, while still a schoolboy, heard Sir Arthur lecture, and over the following years, he and many other scholars worked on the problem. Few of the tablets discovered by Evans had been published—only 160 out of 3000. Then, new tablets written in the same script were discovered at Pylos, and in 1951,

and 1952, these, and the rest of Evans' tablets were published. In the latter year Ventris and his colleagues, especially his friend and close collaborator, John Chadwick, were able to test their theory that the scripts were a form of early Greek. In his and Chadwick's historic work, *Documents in Mycenaean Greek,* they published the results of their work.

The conclusion arrived at by Ventris is generally accepted by scholars today, and it raises a host of questions about previously held ideas. For if Linear B script is in Greek, and if the dating of the tablets at 1400 B.C. is correct, Greek-speaking people must have been ruling at Knossos in the fifteenth century B.C. Or, if the tablets were written by Mycenaeans who had come over from the mainland, it can hardly be they who burned the Cretan palaces at this time.

The tablets on which there were hieroglyphics and Linear A script are believed to be earlier forms of Linear B. The documents themselves are disappointing in that they contain no literature, but only lists and inventories

Helmeted soldiers carrying lances and round shields on this jar known as the Warrior Vase attest to the warlike temperament of the ancient Greeks.

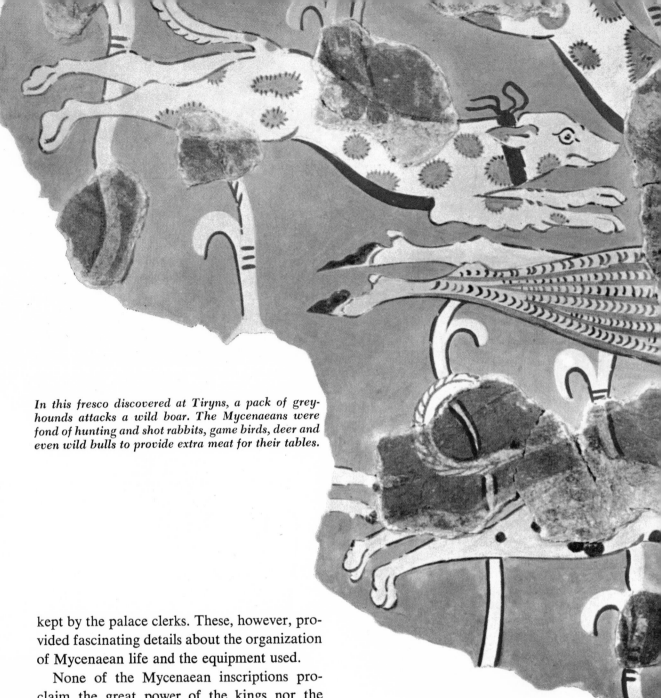

In this fresco discovered at Tiryns, a pack of grey-hounds attacks a wild boar. The Mycenaeans were fond of hunting and shot rabbits, game birds, deer and even wild bulls to provide extra meat for their tables.

kept by the palace clerks. These, however, provided fascinating details about the organization of Mycenaean life and the equipment used.

None of the Mycenaean inscriptions proclaim the great power of the kings nor the supreme might of the gods. There are, however, various references to well-known names, such as Hector, and to such gods as Poseidon, Zeus, Hera, Athena and Hermes. But the records of land tenure, food supplies, taxation, heads of sheep and cattle, amounts of oil, wine, and grain, indicate a complex and tightly organized society.

At the end of the thirteenth century B.C., the great Mycenaean palaces, such as those at Pylos, Tiryns, and Iolkos, were burned to the ground, and were never rebuilt. At Tiryns,

buried beneath the charred debris of the city walls, the skeletons of the last defenders lay where they fell. Among the Linear B tablets found at Pylos are some which suggest preparation for an impending attack: watchers are posted to guard the coast, ships' crews are sent off on naval business, and so on. There are, however, no written records of the actual catastrophe, and only the mute stones bear witness to whatever took place.

The last wave of invading Greeks were, according to historians, the Dorians, an illiterate people who came from the northwestern regions, passing through central Greece and occupying the Peloponnesus by the twelfth century B.C.

At about the same time, hordes of migrants were pouring down the coasts of Syria and Palestine, and on to Egypt, where they were met and thrown back by Ramesses III. Shortly before, the great Hittite empire in Anatolia had collapsed under the assault of thousands of invaders.

Many Mycenaeans fled from their Dorian overlords and eventually settled in Asia, south of Troy and on the nearby islands. One great Mycenaean city, Athens, had escaped destruction by the Dorians, and the refugees poured into it before they crossed the Aegean Sea into the new land, which came to be called Ionia.

A Military Historian and An Ancient Baedeker Comment on the Early Greeks

This little figure was a votive offering, and probably represents a worshiper.

A detail from a gold cup shows a wild bull being decoyed by a cow so that he may be captured by a herdsman.

THUCYDIDES HAD COMMANDED AN ATHENIAN ARMY DURING THE PELOPONNESIAN WAR WHICH RAGED THROUGHOUT THE HELLENIC WORLD IN THE FIFTH CENTURY B.C. HIS HISTORY OF THAT STRUGGLE DESCRIBES AN AGE AS TURBULENT AS THE DAWN OF GREEK CIVILIZATION, WHEN THE FIRST HELLENIC SETTLERS ARRIVED IN THE LAND:

ON GREECE'S EARLIEST INHABITANTS: ". . . the country now called Hellas had in ancient times no settled population; . . . migrations were of frequent occurrence, the several tribes readily abandoning their homes under the pressure of superior numbers . . . never planting their land (for they could not tell when an invader might not come and take it all away, and when he did come they had no walls to stop him), they cared little for shifting their habitation, and consequently neither built large cities nor attained to any form of greatness. The richest soils were always most subject to this change of masters. . . . The goodness of the land favored the aggrandizement of particular individuals, and thus created faction which proved a fertile source of ruin. It also invited invasion. Accordingly Attica, from the poverty of its soil enjoying freedom from faction, never changed its inhabitants. . . . The most powerful victims of war or faction from the rest of Hellas took refuge with the Athenians as a safe retreat; and at an early period, becoming naturalized, swelled the already large population of the city to a height that Attica became at last too small to hold them, and they had to send out colonies to Ionia.

THE POWER OF MYCENAE: "Now Mycenae may have been a small place, and many of the towns of that age (the time of Agamemnon) may appear comparatively insignificant. . . . And yet they occupy two-fifths of the Peloponnesus and lead the whole, not to speak of their numerous allies without . . . the city is neither built in a compact form nor adorned with magnificent temples and public edifices, but composed of villages after the old fashion of Hellas . . . but we may safely conclude that the armament surpassed all before it. . . . (Homer) has represented it as consisting of twelve hundred vessels. . . .

PIRACY: "For in early times the Hellenes and the barbarians of the coast and islands, were tempted to turn pirates. . . . the motives being to serve their own cupidity and to support the needy. They would fall upon a town unprotected by walls, and consisting of a mere collection of villages, and would plunder it; indeed, this came to be the main source of their livelihood, no disgrace being yet attached to such an achievement, but even some glory."

Some of the cups and vases of the Minoan potters were so delicate that they were covered with painted designs to strengthen the fragile pottery as well as decorate it.

PAUSANIAS' ANCIENT GUIDEBOOK, "DESCRIPTION OF GREECE," WAS WRITTEN IN THE SECOND CENTURY A.D. THE GREEK TRAVELER SUPPLEMENTED HIS ROAD GUIDE WITH OBSERVATIONS ON THE SIGHTS AND MONUMENTS OF ART THAT COULD BE SEEN ALONG THE WAY.

THE FOUNDING OF MYCENAE: "The Greeks are aware that the founder of Mycenae was Perseus, so I will narrate the cause of its foundation and the reason why the Argives afterward laid Mycenae waste. . . .

"On its site the cap (*myces*) fell away from (Perseus') scabbard. and he regarded this as a sign to found a city. . . . He was thirsty, and the thought occurred to him to pick up a mushroom (*myces*) from the ground. Drinking with joy water that flowed from it, he gave to the place the name of Mycenae. Homer in the *Odyssey* mentions a woman Mycenae in the following verse: 'Tyro and Alcmene and the fair-crowned lady Mycene.' She is said to have been the daughter of Inachus . . . they say that this lady has given her name to the city."

This ceremonial axe or macehead, made in the shape of a running leopard, is decorated with the spiral pattern so common in Minoan art.

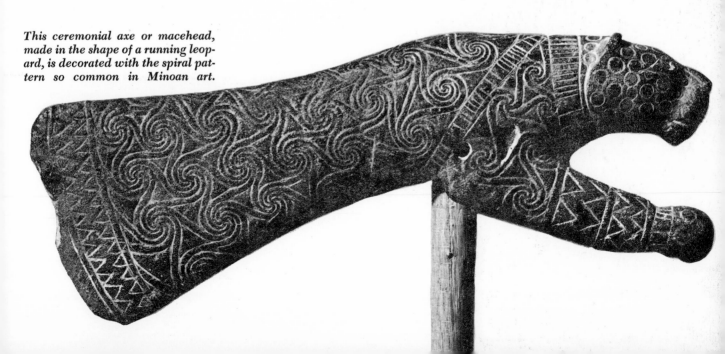

THE VANISHED WORLDS OF ANATOLIA

ANATOLIA was the home of the Hittites who, between 2000 and 1000 B.C., were one of the great civilized powers of the ancient world. Occupying an enormous peninsula between Europe and Asia, Anatolia was a great land bridge between the two continents. The western coast borders on the Aegean Sea and has the warm, sunny climate, the olive groves and the vineyards of the Mediterranean lands. The southern coast grows cotton and citrus fruits.

Huge masonry walls once protected the Hittite cities of Anatolia against invaders. From a wall that guarded Alaja Huyuk the sphinx gateway at left still stands.

Much of the Black Sea coast is semi-tropical, but the eastern mountains have an alpine climate like that of Switzerland.

The great mountain ranges that cover much of this land have had a telling effect on the course of Anatolian history. They presented almost impassable barriers to the imperial Roman legions, and at the same time, prevented much intermingling among the native Anatolians themselves. Parts of Anatolia are like a raging sea turned to stone; peaks and massifs rear up on every side, tumbling to the restless horizon. This violent landscape, fit home for mysterious gods and peoples, is ut-

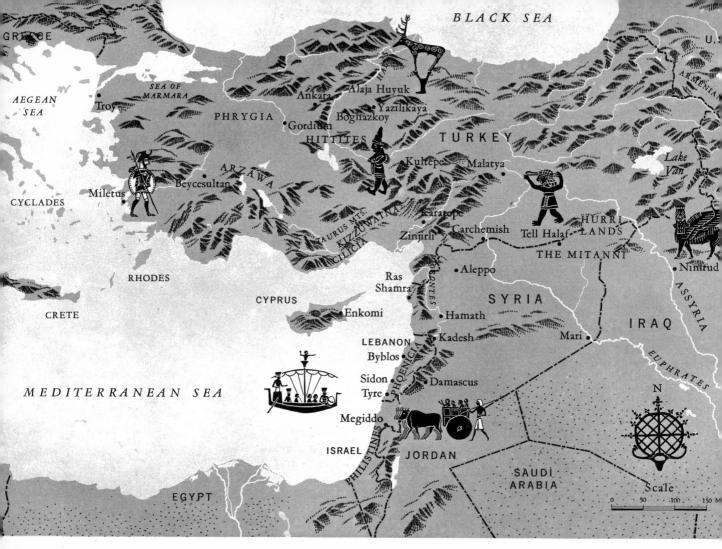

Anatolia, the ancient name of Asia Minor, was the home of the Hittites; the peninsula served as a two-way land bridge that connected Europe and Asia.

terly unlike the monotonous plains of the Tigris and Euphrates or the Indus, or the fertile valley of the Nile.

Anatolia remains the least-known sector of that part of the world which nourished the earliest civilizations. For 500 years it was the heart of the Ottoman Empire, a territory to which few Europeans were admitted. Even after the rebellion in the twentieth century under Ataturk, few foreigners found easy access to the country.

In one way, at least, this isolation proved fortunate, for the ancient ruins of Anatolia remained free from the indiscriminate plundering that destroyed so much of archaeological value in Egypt and Mesopotamia.

The search for the lost world of the Hittites was one of the most fascinating treasure hunts in the whole history of archaeology. Investigators found their first clues in biblical references to these ancient people. (One of the best-known stories of the Old Testament is that of King David and Bathsheba, who was the wife of Uriah the Hittite.) But the search was confused by the fact that the Hittites of the Bible were not the same people as the Hittites who had earlier fought with the Egyptians. As we know, Egyptian temple reliefs commissioned by Ramesses II illustrated the pharaoh's battles with the "abominable Kheta" as he once termed the Hittites. Another inscription recorded that in the year 1280 B.C., Ramesses signed a treaty with the Hittite king Hattusilis III.

Nineteenth and twentieth century explorers were sure that the Hittites of the Hebrews, the Kheta of the Egyptians, as well as the Hatti of the Assyrians were all the same people. But who were they? And where did they live—where had they come from?

As archaeologists and scholars began their search, the name Hittite kept cropping up in one form or another again and again. In Mesopotamia an inscription dating from 1100 B.C. described how the Assyrian king came to know a powerful kingdom called Great Hatti.

As in Sumer and in Crete, the discovery of an unknown form of writing was the first major clue. Two blocks of basalt, found in Syria at different times in the nineteenth century, were covered with heiroglyphic writing which resembled no known language. Linguists could make nothing of them until, in 1876, A. H. Sayce, a famous Assyriologist, announced that he believed both blocks to be inscribed in the Hittite language. He subsequently identified rock inscriptions found in several other Syrian towns, as being in this language, too. By this time, many more explorers made expeditions into the still dangerous hinterland of Anatolia. The country was difficult to travel in, and extremely inhospitable. Excitement grew as each explorer brought back reports of inscriptions, sculptures, and even the ruins of cities high up in the central plateaus of Anatolia.

Most impressive, they reported, were the great sculptured reliefs showing men similar in appearance to the Kheta of the Egyptian temples! Later, another clue turned up in far-off Egypt. A peasant woman came upon large quanties of baked clay tablets which, when they finally came into the hands of authorities, proved to be letters addressed in the Akkadian language to the pharaoh by some of his Syrian and Palestinian vassals, warning him of a menacing nation to the north. There were also two letters written in an unknown language.

The search for the Hittites continued amid such tantalizing clues, and in 1906, Hugo Winkler, a German archaeologist, began excavations at Boghazkoy, a town in Turkey, in search of more tablets. Above the town was a

slight rise on which stood the ruins of an ancient city. The ruins, and the weatherworn sculptures of men and animals that still remained there, were well-known to archaeologists. But Winkler had come to search for tablets, and when he dug a wide trench to the top of the citadel mound, he came upon an exciting discovery. His excavators struck what had evidently been a palace archive, which contained over ten thousand tablets, all in cuneiform writing, including many in the mysterious language, which was referred to at that time as Arzawa. But besides these, there were tablets in Akkadian, which could, of course, be read. Was it possible that this was the capital city of Arzawa—perhaps the capital city of the elusive Hittites?

It was indeed possible, and before too long, the tablets were deciphered and the long-silent Hittites were able to speak again of their life and culture.

After Winkler's discoveries, Anatolia became an archaeological Mecca. As a result, many of the mysteries concerning these people have been cleared up, and the story of the rise

Four-thousand-year-old business transactions were recorded in cuneiform writing on clay tablets which were then inserted in seal-impressed clay envelopes.

and fall of a great civilization has been unfolded.

Parts of Anatolia began to be occupied by humans as far back as 5000 B.C. But the oldest city that has yet been excavated is Troy, whose great period occurred around 2400 B.C. At that time, Troy had a monumental fortress with mansions, and a high civilization with a rich and sophisticated art.

Troy was first excavated by Heinrich Schliemann, the rich and eccentric amateur archaeologist, who believed that the jewelry he discovered there was the "Treasure of Priam." Actually, studies proved that the jewelry dates from the Early Bronze Age, about 1000 years before the traditional date of the Trojan War.

Fairly recently, another such richly filled burial was discovered at Dorak, near the Sea of Marmara. Also from the Bronze Age, the tombs contained the bodies of a local ruler and his wife, the king's favorite hunting dog, food offerings, and beautifully made ceremonial weapons. Behind one body were four axeheads made of amber, lapis lazuli, obsidian, and nephrite, and decorated with gold and silver. The queen had been buried with her jewelry and a silver-handled scepter. The household treasures of these Early Bronze Age rulers included vases, jugs, and bowls of gold and silver. But the most remarkable discovery was part of a gold-encased throne; finely drawn on it was the cartouche of the Old Kingdom Egyptian pharaoh, Sahure. The throne may have been a

gift, or more likely, it was acquired in trade. However it got there, the throne enabled its discoverers to date the tomb around 2500 B.C., which was about 500 years before the Hittites moved into Asia Minor.

Other recent discoveries have disclosed even richer finds dating from the Early Bronze Age period. Under the ancient Hittite city of Alaja Huyuk a series of elaborate tombs, not unlike the Mycenaean shaft graves, was discovered. The quality of the ornaments and jewelry was as high as that of the Sumerian metalwork found in the death pits of Ur. The tombs also yielded vigorous animal sculptures of bronze bulls and stags, reminiscent of the art of the nomadic tribes of the Asian steppes.

Other discoveries show a similarity to Mycenaean architectural styles, suggesting that the Minoans and Mycenaeans may indeed have originated in Anatolia. Scholars have different opinions on this matter.

One thing about these early people appears clear, however. They lived in fairly small communities under a ruling aristocracy. There was as yet no unified state with a common social and economic system, as in Egypt or Babylonia.

The ancestors of the Hittites entered Anatolia early in the second millennium B.C., and like the Mycenaeans, the Hittites found a Bronze Age people living in the land they invaded. Conquest and unification were slow, due to the mountainous nature of the land.

During the reign of Hattusilis I, the Hittites began to spread southward and two generations later, they conquered Babylon, in about 1600 B.C. In the fifteenth century B.C., the Hittites battled with the Hurrians who lived in an area between the northern Tigris and Euphrates. The Hurrians were defeated, although not by the Hittites, but by the great warrior pharaoh Tuthmosis III who had led his conquering armies through northern Syria. This may have been the first contact between Egypt and the new nation of mountain dwellers.

During the reigns of the Egyptian pharaohs Amenhotep III and IV (Akhenaten), an Indo-European group called the Mitanni had taken over the Hittites' old enemies, the Hurrians. The Mitanni entered into friendly relations with the Egyptians, but began to harass the Hittites. Two Hittite kings of this period struggled unsuccessfully against the Mitanni; but when the great Suppiluliumas became king of the Hittites, the Mitanni were vanquished. Recovering his lost provinces, Suppiluliumas sacked the Mitannian capital. Again the Hittite armies began to roll southward, reaching areas where Egyptian influence was strong. One of the Egyptian vassals, the king of Kadesh, offered battle and was roundly defeated in a terrifying assault by the Hittite charioteers. Suppiluliumas, carried forward by the impetus of his advance, pressed on into the Levant. Far from their mountain

The golden scabbard at left shows a mixture of Syrian and Egyptian motifs. The method of metalworking shown in the crescent-bladed axe at right is Syrian, an area which exchanged many cultural influences with Anatolia.

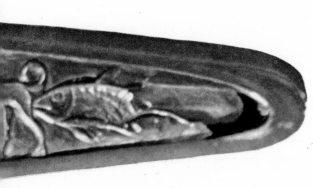

homeland, the Hittites now turned their gaze southward toward the gates of Egypt. The time of the Hittite advance was about 1370 B.C.

The rough mountain men were now encamped in Lebanon. From the surrounding regions, Syrian kings, former vassals of Egypt, came to the tent of Suppiluliumas, bearing tribute. And a few hundred miles to the south lay the greatest power on earth, with a civilization stretching back more than 1500 years to a time when the ancestors of the Hittites may have been only skin-clad barbarians living in a Stone Age society.

The mountain armies spent the next thirty years in long and hard campaigning. At the end of that time, Suppiluliumas was an old man; he had fought with the Assyrians and had consolidated his hold on Syria. One day, a messenger arrived at the tent of the king, carrying a letter—on one of the familiar clay tablets—from Egypt.

The letter was from the queen of Egypt, then a young girl of no more than sixteen years. She wrote to the old warrior, "My husband has died, and I have no son, but of you it is said that you have many sons. If you would send me one of your sons, he could become my husband. I will on no account take one of my subjects and make him my husband. I am very much afraid."

This letter was found by Winkler among the archives of Hattusas, the Hittite capital. Unfortunately, there were no copies of the king's reply, but from Egyptian and Hittite records, we have been able to piece together the rest of the story.

The young Egyptian queen was undoubtedly the widow of Tutankhamen, the boy-pharaoh who died when he was about eighteen. According to Egyptian custom, another man could ascend the throne only by marrying the widow of the dead pharaoh. Surrounded by intriguing, power-hungry courtiers and politicians, the young queen was apparently looking desperately for an escape.

Suppiluliumas did, apparently, send one of his sons, but the plan was never completed, for the young man was murdered en route to Egypt, and records show that the next king of Egypt was Ay, an elderly politician who had been Tutankhamen's chief minister.

By the time of Suppiluliumas' death, the Hittite empire, stretching from Anatolia to southern Syria, had become the chief rival power of Egypt. And in 1300 B.C., the two finally clashed. Ramesses II led the Egyptians, and after a terrible battle, the pharaoh claimed a complete victory. This was the great battle that Ramesses had commemorated in the huge and detailed reliefs carved on the temple walls at Thebes.

Later, however, Ramesses signed a treaty with a subsequent Hittite king, and even, as we know, married a Hittite princess.

The Hittite tablets tell us little about the ordinary people and the way in which they lived. From the pictures they left, they appear to have been a short, stocky, broad-shouldered folk who wore long woolen robes and boots with upturned toes as a protection against the winter snows. Their main cities were built on easily defended hills, with strong walls and towers. They were apparently clever strategists and tough fighters, but unlike the Assyrians, accorded their defeated foes humane treatment.

As in Egypt, there were many regional religious cults. The king was the high priest of the state religion. Many rock-cut sculptures depict the various deities—the most important of whom were the weather god Teshub, and his consort Hebat. It is natural that the Hittites who lived in a land subject to frequent violent storms should make their most important god the one who controlled the thunder and lightning, just as in Egypt, the people who lived under the cloudless skies made Re, the sun god, their chief diety.

The Hittites borrowed much of their art, culture, and religion—and a convenient writing system—from their more highly developed Mesopotamian neighbors, but they come to life in their surviving documents as rugged, independent people, energetic and adventurous. They lived by agriculture, stock-raising, and the trade of copper, silver, and iron. The smelting of iron was to revolutionize the ancient world, and the technique of producing it in commercial quantities is believed to have originated in Asia Minor. The Hittites however, remained essentially a Bronze Age people.

About the same time that iron began to be used for weapons and tools in the twelfth century B.C., the tribes of Asia Minor were jostled about by waves of invaders. The Hittites were swept down from the mountains into the hills of northern Syria, and gradually became intermingled and obscured by the various cultures of other peoples.

In Anatolia, however, during the centuries following 1200 B.C., a new people emerged. These were the Phrygians, an Iron Age people, who gave their name to conical hats which later came to be a symbol of revolution. The Phrygians have been best remembered for their king, Midas of the golden touch, and for their capital city, Gordium, where Alexander cut the Gordian knot. At Gordium, American archaeologists have recently discovered a royal sepulcher, possibly the tomb of King Midas, who according to Greek tradition, died around 680 B.C. Whether or not this was the legendary king's tomb cannot be determined but no scrap of gold was found although the sepulcher was full of objects of bronze and rare woods.

Our knowledge of both Hittite and Phrygian history is far from complete. The Hittite hieroglyphic has still not been completely deciphered although now it is simply a matter of time. New archaeological discoveries are being made in Asia Minor that will undoubtedly cause revision of some of our current ideas. But at last, Anatolia, a long neglected land of rich interest, is coming into its own.

This pitcher was found on Cyprus, a stop along the trading route between Syria and Egypt.

ETRURIA

the mysterious world

of the etruscans

ETRURIA, the ancient home of the Etruscans, lay on the western side of Italy between the Arno River (which flows through modern-day Florence) and the Tiber, which passes into the sea southwest of Rome. It included all of the region known today as Tuscany, and its colonies extended north as far as the Po Valley and south to the hills around Naples. Many of the most famous cities in Italy were originally Etruscan—Pisa, Arezzo, Cortona, Siena, Volterra, Orvieto, Perugia, Assisi, and others.

One of the most beautiful regions in Italy, the Etruscan countryside has both fertile plains and steep, narrow valleys liberally sprinkled with small rivers—the *torrenti*—which run low in summer, but in a boiling froth of white water in the winter months. Vines, olives, and wheat grow in the lowlands; cattle graze on the lower hills, and sheep and goats are pastured on the higher slopes.

Little over a century ago, however, part of Tuscany was a desolate, barren country. At that time, even though the history of the Etruscans had long been a subject of considerable in-

A terra-cotta sarcophagus shows an Etruscan aristocrat and his wife reclining together on a couch as if attending a banquet in the life hereafter.

The Etruscan homeland lay between the Arno and the
Tiber rivers. Its colonies reached north into the
farmlands of the Po Valley, and south to the hills
around Naples. Many of the most famous Italian cities
were originally Etruscan.

132

vestigation and speculation, Tuscany was, according to the English traveler George Dennis, "a countryside almost decimated by malaria, never crossed by the educated and intelligent traveler, (where) the most striking monuments may rest for centuries without attracting attention. Ruins and remains are such common sights in this country that they excite no particular attention." Most of these ruins were ancient tomb sites—often whole underground streets of sepulchers cut out of the rocks. In the eighteenth and nineteenth centuries, there had been great interest in the ruins, and amateur archaeologists from all over Europe had swarmed through the area in search of artifacts to add to their own collections.

Hundreds of treasures had been discovered in the ancient tombs, and museums and private galleries overflowed with statues of stone, terra cotta or bronze, painted pottery, and gold vessels, lamps, candelabra, mirrors, bracelets, rings, and pendants. These artifacts excited much curiosity and scholarly research for little was known about the Etruscan people. Over 2400 years old, some of the tomb objects resembled Roman forms, while others appeared to have been influenced by Greek art. But they were neither Greek nor Roman; neither were they oriental in origin, although they had much in common with eastern styles. However, even though so many artifacts have been found, and there has been such widespread interest in their creators, the Etruscans have remained a puzzling people up to the present.

Our knowledge of most ancient civilizations is based not only on archaeological remains, but also in large part on the literature of a country. Unfortunately, except for brief inscriptions, none of the Etruscan literature has survived. The inscriptions are in letters much like Greek, and can be read and pronounced, but they are not well understood, as no one has yet been able to decipher the language.

We are not yet sure where the Etruscans came from. One theory, based on an account by Herodotus, states that they were emigrants from Lydia in Asia Minor who left their homeland during a period of great famine. An opposing view is that they were indigenous to Italy, although subject to influences from the East. The dispute still goes on.

Until the first millennium B.C., there were no civilized nations in Italy, or in Western Europe. Primitive tribes of the so-called Bronze Age culture, had lived on the Italian Peninsula for hundreds of years. Then, around 1000 B.C., immigrants—or invaders—people who were familiar with the use of iron, swept down into Italy and established themselves in control of the Tuscan region.

These people grew and flourished around Tarquinia, Cerveteri, and Veii, which later became the centers of Etruscan civilization.

One distinctive cultural development of these early people, known as Villanovan, was

Thousands of tiny granules of gold were carefully fused together by Etruscan goldworkers to make the beard and hair of the river god Achelous.

133

their burial custom. They cremated their dead, placing the ashes in urns or small hut-shaped tombs. These vessels were then buried in pits, along with objects that might be needed by the deceased in the afterlife; men had their bronze and iron weapons, while women were buried with bronze and amber jewels, combs, needles, and spindles.

This period, between 1000 and 750 B.C., corresponds to the Dark Age in Greece, between the collapse of the brilliant civilizations of Crete and Mycenae and the dawn of the classical period. In other parts of the world, Egypt had begun its slow decline, while Assyria was emerging in its second rise to power. In Asia Minor the Phrygians and the Lydians were firmly established. The Phoenicians of the Levant were migrating westward, to establish their great colony at Carthage on the North African coast. The Dorian Greeks were also on the move, in search of new lands and trade.

Towards the end of this period, the Villanovan culture began to show signs of change that anticipated the splendid development of the Etruscan culture in the centuries that followed. The dead were no longer cremated but were interred in vaulted mausoleums, and the grave objects became richer and more numerous. These somewhat resembled Greek shields, helmets and swords in character, but clearly were not Greek in origin.

Aside from the Greek influence certain ideas from the east were transmitted to Etruria. As in the societies of many Eastern peoples, the Etruscans' religion was highly ritualistic and made great use of divination by signs. Such a conception was common in the ancient East but not among the Indo-European peoples of the West. The Etruscans' name for themselves, Rasenna, is found in various forms in Asia Minor. And on the island of Lemnos in the Aegean, archaeologists discovered inscriptions in a language that is remarkably like ancient Etruscan. If, as has been suggested, the Etruscans came from Anatolia, it is likely for them to have lived in Lemnos, which is just a few miles off the coast. And in tomb paintings, women are given an honored place, which was not the attitude of Greeks toward their women, though it was a characteristic of some of the older oriental civilizations.

While not an early influence on the Etruscans, Greek culture certainly made a strong impression in later years. Etruscan aristocrats modeled themselves on the heroes of Mycenae, and the major Etruscan gods were closely identified with those of Greece.

Etruscan artists decorated tombs and vases with scenes from Greek mythology, and as early as the seventh century B.C., there were Greek vase painters working in Cerveteri. The Etruscan alphabet itself is of Greek origin.

Aside from the debatable racial origins of the Etruscans, their culture took on its distinctive form at a time when the Greeks and other migrants from the east were founding colonies and pushing their trading ventures into the western Mediterranean area.

In the struggle for raw materials, in which Greeks contested with Phoenicians, Etruria stood in a key position. The main source of Etruria's wealth and prosperity was her mineral deposits, of which other Mediterranean powers were envious. In the northern part of Etruria were the hills known today as the Colline Metallifere, rich in iron, zinc, tin, and copper. The gold, silver, ivory, and other precious materials that the Etruscans later imported to adorn their bodies, their homes, and eventually their tombs can only have been obtained in exchange for these valuable minerals.

Etruria also had dense forests which both provided timber and sheltered abundant game; the climate was kindly, the plains fertile, and the foothills offered abundant pasturage. There were good harbors, and a long sea coast from which mariners could set out on adventurous journeys to other lands.

We know from the Greeks that the Etruscans were skillful and formidable sailors. One legend tells how Etruscan mariners even succeeded in capturing the Greek god Dionysus, who only escaped by changing his captors into dolphins. In these Greek stories, the Etruscans appear to be ruthless pirates, as no doubt they often were. Such a reputation did not endear the Etruscans to the Greeks, but they prove what a power these pre-Roman rulers of western Italy must have been.

During the period 700 to 500 B.C., the Etruscan coastal cities, such as Cerveteri, Tarquinia, and Vetulonia, sent out fleets which sailed along the coasts of Provence, Spain, and North Africa, mixing legitimate trading with profitable piracy. In doing so they encountered their chief rivals, the Greeks and the Carthaginians, whom they often fought with zest and success. For a short time Etruria dominated the western seas as the Mycenaeans had earlier dominated the Aegean.

But when the Greek colonists began settling in Corsica, the Etruscans allied themselves with Carthage against the Hellenes. After a major naval battle in 540 B.C. the Greeks evacuated Corsica, but though the Etruscans had removed one danger, Carthage profited most from the victory. From then on she dominated the western Mediterranean and guarded the Straits of Gibraltar. Thereafter the Etruscans were mostly confined to the Tyrrhenian Sea.

Their expansion on land, however, was formidable. Between 550 and 500 B.C., their armies crossed the Apennines and the Po Valley. They settled at Bologna, building a great city there, crossed over to the Adriatic, occupied Rimini and Ravenna, and established a thriving port at Spina, which became the entrepôt for valuable trade between the Greeks and the Celtic peoples beyond the Alps. From this trade and their own exports Etruscan merchants grew rich. Many Etruscan bronze and gold objects, as well as products of Greek origin, which were probably traded by the Etruscans to the people farther north, have been found in Switzerland and even Burgundy.

The Etruscan god Tinia was, like Zeus, the ruler of the heavens and the chief of all the gods.

A pair of winged horses harnessed to the chariot of a god adorned the pediment of a temple at Tarquinia. Although the city was sacked by Rome in the fourth century B.C., only the cult images were destroyed, and sculptures such as this one have survived.

Southward they penetrated into Latium and Campania. They occupied the site of Rome, and it was they who made Rome a city. Later tradition recalled that the Etruscan dynasty of the Tarquins ruled Rome between 616 and 510 B.C. and that they were the last kings of ancient Rome before the founding of the Roman Republic. Before they were overthrown, Tyrrhenian soothsayers predicted that Rome would one day be "the head of all Italy," and indeed their predictions came to pass.

Etruria was never an empire united under a strong central government, but rather a loose federation of city-states each under its chief or lord, the *lucumon*, a priest-king.

Eventually the Etruscan monarchies were superseded by oligarchies. Within the Etruscan

league, there were twelve cities, headed by a chief magistrate of the Etruscan nation, who was elected annually.

Although they may have been less gifted as artists and innovators, the Romans had vital qualities that the Etruscans lacked—the capacity not only to rule, but to win and retain the loyalty of the ruled. They also learned how to create a unified state. When Rome began her march to power, she annexed first one and then another piece of Etruscan territory. Then in the fourth century B.C. a new threat appeared from the north when the wild, semi-barbaric Gauls swept down into Italy. Years of fighting and devastation followed, and eventually the Gauls left. After the long battles, the glory of Etruria was over, and not long afterward she had become, like the other Italian peoples, merely part of the Roman Republic.

The Romans learned, borrowed, and inherited much from their Etruscan neighbors and overlords before eliminating them as a cultural and political entity. Etruscan elements survived in the trappings and insignia of office. The Roman toga originated as an Etruscan ceremonial garment. The robe of office of the Etruscan rulers was purple, a color which Romans adopted for a similar purpose and which, indeed, is still today an emblem of royalty.

With the expansion of Roman power, Etruscan customs disappeared, and we can judge what kind of people the Etruscans were only by their remains and by allusions to them in the literature of other peoples. And such allusions, as noted before, were often prejudiced. "The Etruscans raise all children without knowing to whom they belong," wrote the Greek historian Theopompus, in the fourth century B.C. He also made reference to the uninhibited pursuit of pleasure by the Etruscans, and there is some archaeological evidence to support this, in scenes depicted on the walls of the Etruscan tombs. The later Romans too had no scruples about painting orgiastic scenes on the walls of their villas, as at Pompeii. It would be disingenuous to ignore such stories altogether, although they may have been exaggerated. Yet most Greek writers stress the Etruscans' fondness for and indulgence in luxury—a point amply confirmed by the sumptuous paraphernalia that accompanied them to their graves. As the tombs reveal, they were a life-loving people charged with such vigor as the Greeks had reason to complain of.

One sees the earlier Etruscans as sunburned sailors straining at the oars, while the sea foam crashes over the bulwarks and the lookout sights yet another island to explore or plunder. The Etruscan system of roads was as fine as anything achieved in Tuscany by the Romans centuries later—roads engineered to carry heavy traffic, well-drained, and laid out with tunnels and cuts. The lean and muscular armed warriors of grim and inscrutable visage, so familiar in early bronze and terra-cotta figures that have survived, as well as their resplendent and formidable chariots, speak eloquently of their military prowess.

Their cities were usually laid out on a gridiron plan, with two main intersecting thoroughfares. In the center of each city, they dug a circular trench, and this shaft was believed to lead directly to the underworld. It was covered by a great stone, which was lifted up only on the days on which the dead were allowed to ascend to dwell among the living, or when the first fruits of the harvest were deposited underneath it as an offering to the gods. The two main streets of the town crossed at this spot, dividing the area within the walls into quarters. This gridiron plan of the streets had a specific religious meaning; it reflected very closely the Etruscan view of the universe.

The Etruscans believed that the heavens were divided up into quarters, each of which had an occult significance. In the north, at the

The pleasure-loving Etruscans were renowned in the ancient world for their devotion to music and dancing, as illustrated on this fifth century B.C. vase.

very summit of the sky dwelt the king of the gods, Tinia. The east side, to his left, was favorable. The west side, on his right, was less so, and the northwest corner of the heavens had a decidedly malign influence. Diviners or *haruspices*, further divided the skies into sixteenths and assigned a meaning to each portion. These expert diviners could then interpret the future from the direction of lightning during a storm, or from the flight of birds.

Besides the haruspices, there were other priests who officiated at religious ceremonies in the temples. The word "temple" itself is of Etruscan origin. Each temple was divided into three sections, one for each of the major gods of the Etruscan trinity. These were the gods Tinia, Uni, and Menerva, whose Roman analogues were Jupiter, Juno, and Minerva. But

The chimaera was a frightening, fire-breathing monster, part lion, part serpent, and part goat, and was derived from tales of Greek mythology.

there were also demons and spirits of horror and death, which, as the centuries passed, were depicted more and more frequently in the tombs. One of them, the sinister Charun, who obviously took his name from the Greek ferryman of the river Styx, had a horse's ears and a beaked nose, and was armed with a large mallet. With a body the color of decaying flesh, so that he seems a veritable embodiment of a scene of human sacrifice, the figure of Charun was shown towering over the victim, holding an enormous hammer in his hand and his demon's face painted an eerie blue.

Music and dance played a prominent role in Etruscan life. Aristotle is claimed to have said that the Etruscans fought, kneaded dough, and beat their slaves to the sound of the flute. Other ancient writers tell us that music provided an inevitable accompaniment to sacrifices, banquets, boxing matches, and solemn ceremonies, and that the Etruscans even used music to aid them in snaring wild pigs and

stags. Their painted tomb scenes of dancing to music have an abandon and ecstasy never approached in either Greek or Roman art.

The same spirit of warm, exhilarant life appears in the hunting scenes, especially in the idyllic fresco in the Tomb of Hunting and Fishing at Tarquinia. This has a delightful freshness and informality that is lacking in similar scenes from Egypt. A youth leans over the prow of a boat and drops his line, while a dolphin playfully leaps nearby. The oarsman is taking things easy in the stern, while other youths in the boat gesticulate to him. Overhead, startled birds rise in hurried flight. There is no scene in any ancient fresco more enchanting than this one.

And yet there was another, darker side to the Etruscan character, an apparent fascination with pain, cruelty, and death, particularly noticeable during the later and more decadent period of Etruscan history. The Etruscans were a highly religious people, and all aspects of their lives were prescribed by ritual regulations. They appeared to be governed by strict and fearful regard for the divine powers and a constant anxiety lest, by neglect of omens, signs, and rites, these powers should be offended. While the Greeks and Romans also used divination, their philosophic spirit and more objective turn of mind prevented them from allowing themselves to be completely dominated by religious doctrine.

After the fifth century B.C. Etruscan funerary paintings emphasize scenes of massacre, torture, and violent death. The grimmest of these depict what appear to have been the ritual sports that accompanied Etruscan funeral ceremonies, the battles to the death between gladiators, whose blood, the Etruscans believed, would invigorate the souls of the dead. Curiosity about pain, violence, and death, always present in the darker recesses of the human mind, may have been magnified by the Etruscans until it developed into a morbid obsession. There is some evidence that the Etrus-

The gorgon was also Greek in origin; it represented one of three snake-haired sisters who were so hideous that anyone who viewed them was turned to stone.

cans had a certain fatalism about the life of their nation, and now, believing that the time was approaching for its demise, they laid increasing emphasis on the more somber aspects of their religion.

By 250 B.C. Etruria was part of the Roman political system. One hundred years later, inscriptions were being written in Latin, and by the time of Christ, the Etruscan language had died out except among the country people. Roman cities arose on the sites of many Etruscan towns, and others were deserted and never reoccupied. But the cemeteries remain. Though thousands of tombs were plundered and ransacked, others are still intact.

We may one day succeed in understanding the Etruscan language, although all known examples are short inscriptions, mostly funerary. Possibly the long-debated question of Etruscan origins may finally be settled. Until then, however, we can enjoy their vital, exuberant art, admire the craftsmanship of their jewelers, metalworkers, sculptors, and painters. But they themselves, across twenty-five centuries, remain one of the great enigmas of history.

Three Writers Note the Etruscans

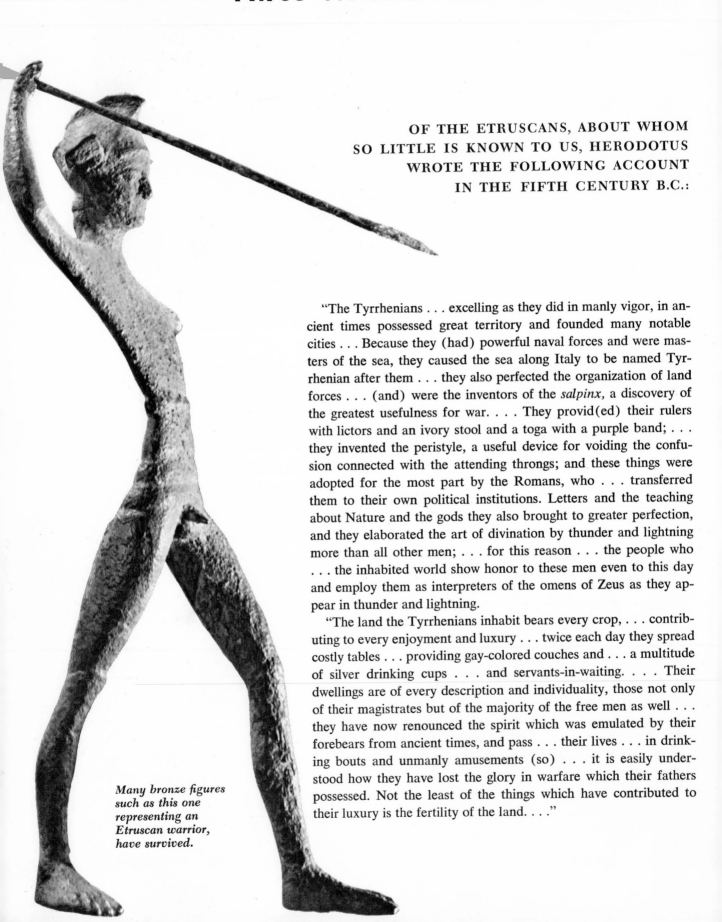

OF THE ETRUSCANS, ABOUT WHOM
SO LITTLE IS KNOWN TO US, HERODOTUS
WROTE THE FOLLOWING ACCOUNT
IN THE FIFTH CENTURY B.C.:

"The Tyrrhenians . . . excelling as they did in manly vigor, in ancient times possessed great territory and founded many notable cities . . . Because they (had) powerful naval forces and were masters of the sea, they caused the sea along Italy to be named Tyrrhenian after them . . . they also perfected the organization of land forces . . . (and) were the inventors of the *salpinx,* a discovery of the greatest usefulness for war. . . . They provid(ed) their rulers with lictors and an ivory stool and a toga with a purple band; . . . they invented the peristyle, a useful device for voiding the confusion connected with the attending throngs; and these things were adopted for the most part by the Romans, who . . . transferred them to their own political institutions. Letters and the teaching about Nature and the gods they also brought to greater perfection, and they elaborated the art of divination by thunder and lightning more than all other men; . . . for this reason . . . the people who . . . the inhabited world show honor to these men even to this day and employ them as interpreters of the omens of Zeus as they appear in thunder and lightning.

"The land the Tyrrhenians inhabit bears every crop, . . . contributing to every enjoyment and luxury . . . twice each day they spread costly tables . . . providing gay-colored couches and . . . a multitude of silver drinking cups . . . and servants-in-waiting. . . . Their dwellings are of every description and individuality, those not only of their magistrates but of the majority of the free men as well . . . they have now renounced the spirit which was emulated by their forebears from ancient times, and pass . . . their lives . . . in drinking bouts and unmanly amusements (so) . . . it is easily understood how they have lost the glory in warfare which their fathers possessed. Not the least of the things which have contributed to their luxury is the fertility of the land. . . ."

Many bronze figures such as this one representing an Etruscan warrior, have survived.

PLINY THE ELDER, THE ROMAN NATURALIST
AND WRITER OF THE FIRST CENTURY A.D.,
TOOK NOTE OF THE ETRUSCANS'
REPUTATION AS SOOTHSAYERS, IN HIS
VOLUME, *NATURAL HISTORY*:

"The Tuscan writers (the Etruscans) hold the view that there
are nine gods who send thunderbolts. . . . Tuscany believes that
some also burst out of the ground, which it calls 'low bolts' and
that these are rendered exceptionally direful and accursed by the
season of winter. . . . The first (thunderbolts) that occur after a
man sets up house for himself are called 'family meteors' as fore-
telling his fortune for the whole of his life. However, people think
that private meteors, except those that occur either at a man's first
marriage or on his birthday, do not prophesy beyond ten years, nor
public ones beyond the thirtieth year, except those occurring at
the colonization of a town."

*In early Etruscan tombs, funerary
urns such as this one have been discovered; because souls were sometimes thought of as dwarflike, ashes
were placed in such human-headed
containers which were then dressed
as dolls. The later gravestone below
shows a woman riding to the underworld in a chariot.*

ANOTHER GREEK HISTORIAN, DIONYSIUS
OF HALICARNASSUS, DISCUSSED THE
POSSIBLE ORIGINS OF THE ETRUSCANS.
IN HIS "ROMAN ANTIQUITIES," COMPOSED
AROUND THE TIME OF CHRIST:

"Some declare (the Etruscans) to be natives of Italy, but others
call them foreigners. Those who make them a native race say that
their name was given them from the forts, which they were the first
. . . to build; for covered buildings enclosed by walls are called by
the Tyrrhenians as well as by the Greeks *tyrseis* or 'towers.'

"But those who relate a legendary tale about their having come
from a foreign land say that Tyrrhenus, who was the leader of the
colony, gave his name to the nation, and that he was a Lydian by
birth. . . .

"I do not believe . . . that the Tyrrhenians were a colony of the
Lydians; for they do not use the same language as the latter (and)
they neither worship the same gods as the Lydians nor make use of
similar laws or institutions. . . . The Romans, however, give them
other names: from the country they once inhabited, named Etruria,
they call them Etruscans. . . ."

CAMBODIA

the land of the khmers

ABOUT a hundred years ago a French explorer named Henri Mouhot was traveling in the Far East in what was then one of the most remote countries in the world. Deep in the jungles of this alien land he came upon an astonishing sight: before him lay an ancient temple city with dazzling towers, richly sculptured walls, and rows of columns and carved figures of smiling Buddhas. The vast temples, lakes, and terraces were, to Mouhot, "far more grandiose

The roots of banyan and silk-cotton trees still hold many Khmer shrines in their grasp; the temple ruin at left stands outside the ancient Cambodian capital.

than anything built in the heyday of Greek or Roman art . . ."

Even more astonishing to the French explorer was the discovery of such glory buried in the tropical jungle among people who had only vague memories of the significance of these buildings. When Mouhot asked who had built them, the Cambodians replied,

"They built themselves."

"We owe these buildings to the Leper King."

"It is the work of giants" (as the Dorian Greeks had said of the ruins of Mycenae).

Mouhot did not know that he had come upon the temple tomb of Angkor Wat, perhaps the

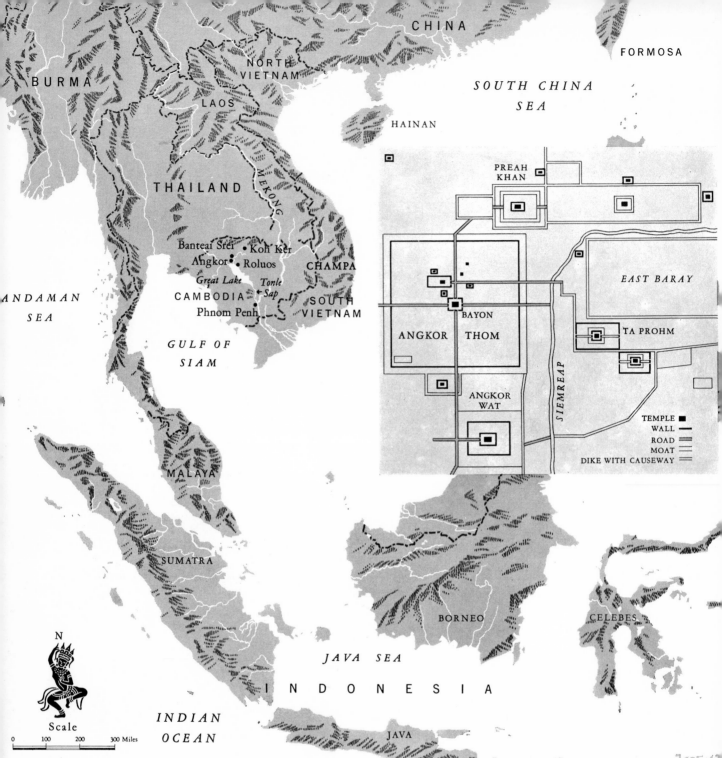

Cambodia was covered with temples, cities, and systems of moats and canals, for not only was every monarch obligated to construct a new temple complex when he ascended the throne, but the building of shrines was also done by members of the royal court.

146

Khmer women were esteemed for their intellect as well as their physical beauty. The apsaras or celestial dancers like this one were often depicted in Khmer art.

finest achievement of the Khmer civilization, which for centuries had flourished so brilliantly in Cambodia, finding its highest expression in art and architecture.

Although it, and the neighboring temple city of Angkor Thom, were abandoned to the jungle only five hundred years ago, they recall an age that is millenniums away from us in spirit, for their builders were inspired by religious and magical impulses similar to those that raised the lofty ziggurat of Marduk in Babylon and the temple of Amen-Re at Thebes.

When Angkor Thom was built at the turn of the thirteenth century A.D., Europeans were constructing cities of an entirely different kind, with cathedrals such as those of Chartres, Cologne, and Salisbury. Most astonishing of all is the fact that here in Southeast Asia, an area virtually unknown to Europeans at the time, a great civilization was flourishing among people whose techniques of agriculture, irrigation, hydraulic engineering, architecture, sculpture, and metalwork equaled, and occasionally surpassed those of the world's other great ancient civilizations.

Today, the ordinary European or American who views the vast remains of the Khmer civilization may be struck by a sense of mystery, a lack of kinship with the civilization that produced these splendid temple cities. Although they are far closer to us in time than the ruins at Knossos and Mycenae, or the temple tombs of Egypt, the ruins of Angkor Thom and Angkor Wat seem infinitely more remote. Perhaps this is because the Khmer civilization drew its inspiration from India, which until very recently also remained separate from Western culture. The Khmer gods were those of India: Brahma, Vishnu, Siva, and later on, Buddha. Khmer mythology derived directly from that of the Hindus and the Buddhists.

The classic enigmatic faces of Buddhas appear everywhere in Angkor Thom. Yet the civilization created by the Khmers was uniquely their own.

By the beginning of the Christian era, Hindu civilization had not only spread through all of India but had been carried eastward and southward to Burma, Thailand, Malaya, and the Indonesian islands. During this formative period from the first to the sixth centuries A.D. the Khmer kingdom began its rise.

Cambodia was then part of a powerful state, called Funan by the Chinese. By about 550 A.D. a Khmer prince seized control of Funan, and the country became known as Chenla, after the Khmer homeland. The next three centuries were ones of generally successful aggrandizement and consolidation, except for a brief period during which the country was taken over by the neighboring island kingdom of Java. Then, in the eighth century A.D. a new king, Jayavarman II, came to the throne. Ruling for 60 years, he declared his country to be independent of Java and established so strong a foundation for the Khmer empire that it grew and prospered for centuries afterward. At this time, the king became identified with the Hindu god Siva—both "the creator and the destroyer" —and thereafter the Khmer kings were regarded as divine, and were worshiped as deities. As such, they constituted the links between mankind and the spirits of nature, and it was this concept that gave the Khmer civilization its distinctive form.

Throughout much of Cambodian history, the king's divine power was represented by a linga, a sacred stone pillar, that symbolized the creative power of Siva. Each king felt impelled to build larger and larger temples to house the royal linga, and thus titanic works of architecture were created.

A group of priests, hundreds of lesser dignitaries, and even whole villages were dedicated to the maintenance of these temples and to the religious ceremonies that centered about them.

Thus it was that the sacred city of Angkor Thom was built at the end of the twelfth century, and the nearby temple-tomb of Angkor Wat, the most beautiful of all Khmer buildings, was erected by the king Suryavarman II in the first part of the same century. At this time the wealth and power of the Khmer kingdom were at their height. During the same period, few nations in Europe could have rivaled Cambodia.

But it was during the reign of Jayavarman VII, the last great Khmer king, that the civilization flourished most splendidly. Jayavarman established Buddhism as the dominant religion, and his building program made his reign the most productive period of Cambodian art. Under his leadership Cambodia became the strongest state in southeast Asia.

Life in Cambodia in the thirteenth century was probably little different from what it is today. Then, as now, people around the great cities lived by agriculture and fishing. The great lake of Cambodia, the Tonle Sap, is fed by the Mekong River that flows down from the southern Chinese mountains and spans the Indochinese peninsula. The lake abounds with fish, and the river is diverted in a thousand ways to irrigate the flat and fertile plains. Broad fields of rice, millet, and other crops support a considerable population.

Groves of tropical fruits—bananas, pomegranates, and oranges—flourish, and aromatic wood trees—aloe, storax, and sandalwood— grow nearby.

In this tropical climate and marsh-filled land, the Khmers often contracted leprosy, a fact which gives confirmation to the reference to the Leper King who may have built the temples of Angkor.

Wildlife was prolific throughout the land; elephants, tigers, and rhinoceroses were common, and crocodiles inhabited the rivers.

Elaborate ornamentation adorns the shrines of Banteai Srei. The doorways are less than five feet high and are guarded by monkeys and mythical monsters.

A serpent hood once framed this statue of the Muchalinda Buddha, who still sits upon the giant snake coils. Mosslike lichen gives the image a mottled effect.

Snakes were very common and as in many other ancient cultures, they were both worshiped and feared.

Valuable minerals also were plentiful in Cambodia, and Chinese travelers wrote of the country's gold, silver, copper, and tin, as well as of ivory, pearls, coral, and glass.

Several accounts, written by Chinese travelers of the time, give us colorful and charming pictures of how the Khmers lived and what the people looked like. To Chou Ta-kuan, a Chinese envoy who regarded them rather critically, all Cambodians looked alike, although one could distinguish the aristocrats because their skins were "as white as jade" since they never went out in the sun. A person's rank could be told by the size and grandeur of his dwelling. The king's palace was roofed with lead tiles, those of the nobles with clay, and the common houses with thatch.

One legend tells of the origin of the Khmer costume and hair-dressing:

In early times, Funan had a woman for a ruler. Her name was Willow-leaf and she was celebrated for her strength and beauty. She clad herself "only in sunbeams" until, successfully courted by a young man with a divine bow and arrow, she married. Her husband regarded her nakedness as barbaric, however, and designed a loose garment for the queen and her subjects, also making her put her hair up in a knot.

Another Chinese writer notes that in the pre-Khmer period, it was "the custom of the inhabitants to go about always armored and under arms." "The least quarrel entails bloody combats . . . the men are small and black but many women are white. All roll up their hair in a chignon and wear ear pendants. They are of a lively and robust temperament . . . They make ablutions each morning, clean their teeth . . . and . . . read or recite their prayers."

The life of the court was centered around the king. One inscription tells us that the Khmer ruler was "the repository of all virtues" and "so superior to other men that he remained "unmoved by the delights of kingship which drive other monarchs mad with joy."

Hundreds of courtiers surrounded the king, and besides the queen and other royal wives, there were concubines and dancing girls, and an all-female bodyguard.

According to Chou Ta-kuan, the highest dignitaries used "palanquins with gold shafts and four parasols with gold handles." Lesser dignitaries had fewer parasols, and conveyances with silver shafts, and the next rank below may have carried only "a silver-handled parasol. The parasols are made of a red Chinese taffeta, and their fringes hang down to the ground."

The main occupation of this horde of officials was the administration of the land, and the control over the dikes and irrigation canals that gave the land its immense fertility. Indeed, inscriptions praise the monarchs who "made the water flow where before there was little or none . . . a reservoir as beautiful as the moon to refresh mankind and drown the insolence of other kings."

There was, however, a wide gulf between the official classes and the ordinary people. The peasants had a house, Chou Ta-kuan reported, but no furniture or utensils. They used clay pots for cooking and coconut shells for ladles. A folded leaf was shaped into a cup for serving rice and sauce. In the homes of the wealthy, however, the Chinese envoy observed that there were fine cups of silver and gold. Women controlled much of the commercial life, and did their trading from little straw mats spread out on the ground in the market place.

OVERLEAF: *Angkor Wat is the supreme example of the Khmer temple-mountain, and is almost supernatural in its beauty. It was the meeting place of kings and gods, and also was the earthly home of the gods.*

By the end of the thirteenth century, the Khmer empire was beginning to disintegrate, for over the centuries the country's wealth had been depleted both by frequent wars with neighboring lands and by the Cambodian kings' mania for building. Now, the nation was further weakened by wars with Siam, and threatened by the Mongol kings of China. In the fifteenth century another raid by the Siamese coincided with the death of the Cambodian king, and the defection of many nobles and priests, and the city of Angkor was finally abandoned. Perhaps, also, the conversion of the Khmer people to Buddhism, with its disregard of human endeavor, played a part in the disintegration and downfall of this once-splendid civilization.

Sculpture and architecture are nearly all that is left of the glorious Khmer achievement. Perhaps no other group of buildings in the world has such richness of decoration, complexity, and sheer size.

The temples were the homes of the gods, and were adorned with guardian deities, figures of dancing girls, and garlands of flowers. Along the whole length of Angkor Wat are statues of the dancing girls or *apsaras,* elephants, and warriors, and candid little scenes from everyday life.

The years during which Angkor Wat was built were of the classic age of Khmer art. A few centuries later, architecture was dominated by a desire for colossal size, although sculpture was more naturalistic than it had been in earlier times. At Angkor Thom an enormous temple called the Bayon was topped with fifty or more towers, each of which had its sides modeled in the shape of a gigantic face representing the king. Outside the gates of Angkor Thom stood other figures, rows of giants carved in stone and holding an enormous serpent in their arms. The gates themselves were supported by the massive figures of two three-headed elephants. One terrace within the town had a pro-

cession of elephants carved along the walls, extending for 1500 feet.

No epic poems, hymns, personal letters, or legal codes have come down to us from Angkor, and we know little of what these people thought, or of their personal trials and triumphs. The hundreds of carved reliefs, however, show us the king and his courtiers at a palace festival, warriors in chariots and on foot, engaging their enemies or leading their captives away. Warships clash in naval battles, fish swim endlessly across the carved panels. Fishermen drop their nets in the Tonle Sap, and peasant women sit in the market place, while youths play at gambling games.

Nearby, a statue of a god-king sits in unearthly repose, having achieved Nirvana, the Buddhist state of perfect blessedness. And not far away are the dancing apsaras, symbols of a more ancient religion, whose ritual movements still beckon and entice in the dances of Southeast Asia today.

The temple wall relief shown at far left illustrates the Cambodian story of the leper king who became contaminated by drops of serpent blood which spattered upon him as he wrestled with a giant snake. The relief above tells of a damsel sent by the gods to divert two demons who were disrupting the world. Below, demons hold a giant snake to form a railing on a causeway approaching Angkor Thom.

A Chinese Diplomat's Views of the Khmers

CHOU TA-KUAN, AN ENVOY FROM
THE CHINESE COURT TO ANGKOR, WROTE
A LIVELY IF SOMEWHAT PATRONIZING
ACCOUNT OF LIFE IN CAMBODIA DURING
THE YEARS IN WHICH THE KHMER EMPIRE
WAS STILL FLOURISHING:

ANGKOR THOM: "Six or seven miles of walls surround the city, which may be entered by five gates. . . . Just outside the walls there is a broad moat beyond which there are causeways with enormous bridges. On both sides of the bridges there are fifty-four stone divinities, looking like generals, terrible and gigantic. . . . The bridges have stone parapets, carved in the form of nine-headed serpents; and the fifty-four divinities hold the serpent in their hands as though to prevent it from escaping. . . . The walls form a perfect square, at

The Khmers' impulse to build temple after temple was perhaps their most striking trait. The bronze figure here is said to represent the "celestial architect."

Moss and creeping vines cover these meditating figures, believed to be attendants of Buddha.

the corners of which rise four stone towers. Marking the center of the kingdom is a tower of gold, surrounded by more than twenty stone towers and hundreds of stone cells. On the east side two golden lions flank a golden bridge, and eight Buddhas of gold are placed at the foot of stone cells.

About a third of a mile north of the golden tower there is a bronze tower, even higher, from which the view is magnificent. At the foot there are ten or more small stone houses. Still another third of a mile farther north is the residence of the king, where another golden tower exists in his sleeping apartments. It is all these wonders which we think have inspired merchants to speak glowingly of "rich and noble Cambodia."

Jayavarman VII is believed to have been the greatest of all Khmer kings, and may also have been the legendary Leper King, who turned the country to Buddhism.

CLOTHING: "Everyone, even the prince, men and women alike, wear their hair in a chignon and are bare shouldered. They simply wrap a piece of cloth around their loins over which they drape another larger one when they go outdoors. The type of material depended upon rank; and some that the prince wears are worth three or four ounces of gold. Such material, of course, is the most beautiful in color and workmanship. . . .

"Floral patterns, woven into the cloth, are reserved for the prince. He wears a crown of gold. . . . His neck is hung with nearly three pounds of huge pearls. On his wrists and ankles he wears bracelets, and on his fingers he wears gold rings set with cat's eyes. The soles of his bare feet and his palms are stained with a red drug. Outside, he carries a golden sword in his hand.

CAMBODIAN WOMEN: "Women here age very quickly; probably because they marry and have children before they are old enough. At twenty or thirty, they look like Chinese women of forty or fifty. . . .

At the top of this relief, figures dance on the deck of a junk; the fish indicate the waters of a river; at the bottom of the relief, two kneeling men hold gamecocks while bettors hover over them.

THE INHABITANTS: "The king has five wives, one for his apartment and one for each point of the compass. As for concubines and palace girls, I have heard mentioned that there may be as many as three to five thousand. . . .

"There are female palace attendants of lower status, and they number at least one or two thousand. They all are married and live among the people. But they shave the front part of their hair in the fashion of northern people and place there a vermilion mark, as well as one on each temple. This is their distinctive mark.

JUSTICE: "The king listens to all legal disputes, even minor ones. In cases of a major crime, the criminal is placed in a ditch outside the west gate, and earth and stones are heaped on top of him, and this is the end. Smaller crimes are sometimes punished by toes, fingers, or nose being cut off. Debauchery and gambling are not forbidden. . . ."

THE RIDDLE
OF THE MAYA

DEEP in the rain forests of Central America stand the remains of a once flourishing civilization whose people were simple, almost primitive farmers and yet were possessed of a highly developed system of writing, and a genius for mathematics and astronomy.

The Maya culture took root in the Peten District of Guatemala, and in nearby sections of Mexico and British Honduras. It is for the most part, an inhospitable territory, covered

The ancient stucco portrait opposite represents an idealized classic Maya profile. Marked with traces of red paint, it was found in a tomb at Palenque.

by marshlands and dense forests of towering trees. The climate, especially during the rainy season, is excessively hot and humid.

In this jungle world, between 300 and 900 A.D., the Maya built great ceremonial centers, and did so without the help of metal tools, wheeled vehicles, or any beasts of burden. Around such centers, whose purpose appears to have been exclusively religious, the Maya cleared enough of the forest to plant crops and build their homes. At the bases of their temples they raised huge stelae—sacred monoliths carved with hieroglyphics and pictures of fantastically dressed human figures.

GULF OF MEXICO

UNITED STATES

MEXICO

CUBA

HONDURAS

GUATEMALA

PACIFIC
OCEAN

• Dzibichaltun

YUCATAN

Mayapan

Chichen Itza

• Coba

Uxmal• • Kabah

Tulum

Jaina • PUUC • Sayil • Labna
AREA

QUINTANA
ROO

CHENES —
RIO BEC AREA

CAMPECHE

TABASCO

PETEN
AREA

BRITISH
HONDURAS

CARIBBE
SEA

Palenque

Uaxactun •

• Piedras Negras

Lake
Peten

• Tikal

MEXICO

Yaxchilan •

Tayasal

USUMACINTA

Bonampak •

CHIAPAS

GUATEMALA

Quirigua •

MOTAGUA

• Copan

PACIFIC
OCEAN

Lake
Atitlan

N

HONDURAS

Scale

Kaminaljuyu •

0   25   50

*Classic Maya culture grew up in the Peten Jungle;
regional variations developed to the south, west, and
north. In Yucatan, at Chichen Itza and other nearby
areas, post-classic cities flourished; the last Maya to
surrender to the Spanish lived on Lake Peten.*

The Maya shared many features of their civilization with neighboring Indian groups, such
as the Zapotec and the Olmec or La Venta culture, whose origins, like the Maya's, are also
obscure. There were hundreds of separate
American Indian tribes, all of whose ancestors
originally came over a land bridge from Asia,
across the Bering Straits and into Alaska, some
twelve to seventeen thousand years ago.

160

By 9000 B.C., these migrant hunters were roaming over North America, and eventually, about three or four thousand years later, some of their descendants had reached Central America. As has happened everywhere in the slow process of civilization, these wandering groups gradually settled down and turned to the raising of food crops, and by 2000 B.C., farm villages began to emerge in parts of Central America.

Maya civilization assumed its distinctive form in the complete isolation of its New World home. It reached its greatest heights during those centuries when medieval Europe knew its darkest days. And yet, when the Spanish conquistadores first set foot on the American continent, they saw only the withered bloom of this once hardy and magnificent civilization.

Between 1500 B.C. and 300 A.D., the Maya evolved beyond the level of primitive village life. They cultivated maize, cotton, agave, and other plants, and had learned to make fine pottery and baskets, and to spin fibers to weave into cloth for their garments. They also built rough pyramid-temples with carvings and impressive staircases leading to the summit.

The principal crop of the Maya farmer was maize; indeed, it was the foundation of his economy, and the plant itself was worshiped as a deity.

The Maya probably had greater reverence for this corn god than for all the other deities in their extremely complex group of divinities. Many of these exerted both good and bad influences. The rain god, for example, brought life-giving waters, but also was responsible for the damp rot and the hail that broke plant stalks. Some deities could operate both in the underworld and in the heavens. Many were four gods in one, their aspects being associated with a different point of the compass and a different color. (The four sacred shades in this connection were red, yellow, black, and white—significantly, each shade is the color of a different kind of corn.)

The most benevolent of the deities was Itzamna, the aged god associated with the sun. Ixtab, the goddess of suicide, was another benevolent deity, since death by one's own hand insured a place in the Maya paradise. According to one early Spanish account, the Maya also believed that the men who were killed in war and the women who died in childbirth were also guaranteed a place in the eternal Maya heaven. The god of death was called Ah Puch, and the owl, the Moan bird, and the dog frequently shown with him had sinister meaning as well.

The occult discipline of Maya religion often confounds those who have tried to understand it. Even in Maya times, the ordinary laborer would have had difficulty, although he would have felt close to the deities of the fruitful earth which gave him life. But he accepted what the priest rulers told him—that the gods must have temples for sacrifice and also must have their needs regularly supplied. So, for more than a

The woman on the plaque below performs a blood sacrifice by pulling a cord through her tongue.

thousand years, generations labored in the tropical heat to quarry stone and haul it to the temple site for building the huge pyramid temples. They made great ball courts, too, in which a ceremonial game was played by Maya youths. The cult of this sacred ball game was widespread among the civilizations of the New World, and it survived up to the time of the Spanish conquest throughout the Americas.

What distinguished the civilization of the Maya from all others, ancient or contemporary, was an obsession with the passage of time. Maya intellectual life was almost entirely devoted to the problem of measuring its flow. For them, time was the philosophical and spiritual basis of the universe. According to the Maya's view, history was repeated in endless cycles, which provided an explanation of present events and a forecast of the future. The gods, both good and evil, they believed, controlled these cycles, and the Maya priests became experts with the calendar as well as intermediaries between man and his gods.

The Maya calendar consisted of two parts, one a solar year, and the other, chiefly ceremonial. The solar year was called the *tun*, and was divided into 365 days. It was made up of eighteen divisions of twenty days each, plus one malevolent five-day period. The ceremonial year, computed along with the approximate solar year, had only 260 days, divided into thirteen different periods. Both years combined to form a larger unit of fifty-two years, called a *katun*, somewhat equivalent to our century.

To measure the passage of time, the Maya priests studied the cycles of the sun and the moon, and the planet Venus. The cycles of the Maya calendars interlocked with each other like the meshing cogs of wheels of different sizes, and a part of the priest's duties was to know which particular cogs—or gods—were coming together at any given moment of time, past, present, or future. To determine what influences were at work on any given day, the priests made calculations millions of years into

Blue was a sacred Maya color and the terra cotta figure opposite may represent a priest. The death mask at right was made of jade mosaic and was found in a pyramid tomb.

the past, in one case four hundred million years.

The revolutions of the sun and planets cannot be reduced to round figures. The Maya knew this, and though they had no way of expressing fractions, they somehow managed to keep such accurate records that they could determine the difference between the true solar year and their year of 365 days. So accurate were their calculations that they could predict solar eclipses with precision that compares well with modern astronomy.

Why did the Maya put all this effort into the study of mathematics? Other civilizations used such calculations to divide their lands, measure seasonal flooding, determine crop yields, and keep business records. The Maya did not do any of these. They had no concept of individual property, for example, and they had no

need for such calculations. However, the Maya believed that his entire welfare lay at the mercy of the gods who controlled the natural forces, and only the mathematician-priests could say which particular combination of good and evil influences operated at any particular moment of time.

What did the ceremonial centers such as Copan, Palenque, Uxmal, Tikal, and Uaxactun look like during the classical age of the Maya? At Tikal, archaeologists have found that there were at one time nearly 3000 buildings in a seven-square-mile space. In the center was a wide ceremonial area and on either side were towering, sacred pyramids, on the tops of which, lifted to the heavens, were tiny one-to-three-room temples. To the north was a cluster of smaller pyramid temples and to the south were nearly a score of low, multi-chambered buildings. At some sites, these large ceremonial buildings formed a giant sundial, or were located according to the position of the stars. In their architecture the Maya never mastered the true arch; but they, almost alone among Central American Indians, used the corbeled vault. By this device, each piece of masonry overlaps the one under it until the two topmost pieces of opposing walls meet at the center and are joined by a capstone. Such a ceiling or vault called for understanding the problems of stress and strain in construction. An equal skill in engineering was evident in the broad highways that crossed the jungles, the lakes, and the swampy marshlands.

It is believed that such sites as these were purely religious centers. Peasants who farmed and dwelt in the surrounding countryside labored also to construct the white stucco buildings, providing the setting in which the priests performed their rites. The priests, in return, provided assurances for the future—predictions about all aspects of life, and the sacrifices necessary to propitiate the deities. Classic Maya civilization appears to have been the product of the brilliance of a few priests and the labor of the millions who lived under their control.

There seems to have been a well-defined class system, headed by the *halach uinic,* or "true man." His duties were both secular and sacred, and below him were the hundreds of priests who conducted the ceremonial rites. Lesser chiefs, called *batabs,* dwelt in the smaller communities surrounding the ceremonial centers, and one of their major responsibilities was to see that regular tribute—in the form of food, incense, jade, and coral—was paid to the halach uinic.

Slaves were kept in some kind of servitude, if they were not subjected to the sacrificial knife.

The Maya economy was dependent upon its farmers. Laborers and craftsmen, however, with only limited tools, were able to create astonishing works of art. Figurines and ornaments were exquisitely fashioned of jade, and painting was finely applied to many-colored pottery. Weaving, of sisal fiber, cotton, and feathers, was performed by the women.

In one recently discovered series of murals, found in a temple ruin, there are finely detailed scenes of raids led by the halach uinic, the ceremonial dance that follows, bloodletting procedures, and at the climax, what appears to be a human sacrificial rite.

These scenes show the splendid garments of the upper classes—rich and ornate loin cloths for the men, and sack-like dresses for the women. Priests' raiments were encrusted with beads and shells, and their elaborate headdresses were worked upon wooden frames in the shape of animals or the faces of gods.

In 1949 the Mexican archaeologist Alberto Ruz was clearing the Temple of the Inscriptions at Palenque, one of the loveliest of Maya sites, when he found that one of the floor slabs had fingerholes in it, apparently to facilitate lifting. When the great slab was raised, it disclosed a vaulted staircase that descended into the interior of the temple's pyramid base. At a depth of about sixty feet the excavators found a crude wall, in front of which was an offering of sea shells, pottery, beads, and a pearl. Farther along the passageway, Ruz found the skeletal remains of six persons. But that was not all. After removing another great stone slab, Ruz found a large vaulted chamber whose walls were modeled with figures in stucco relief; and at the center, a magnificent sculptured slab with the remains of jadeite mosaic human heads and slate pendants. The top of the slab was carved to represent a young man, sur-

This old Maya god was thought to cause earthquakes when he moved underground. When incense was burned in his belly, smoke poured forth from his mouth.

rounded by Maya symbols of life and death. A hieroglyphic text indicated a date of around 700 A.D. This five-ton slab proved to be a "sepulcher stone" covering the lid of a great stone sarcophagus.

Within was the skeleton of the priest ruler who was adorned with an incredible array of jewelry. Near his head were a death mask of jadeite (shown on page 163), jade earplugs, a diadem, pendants, and pearls; and he wore a collar and bracelets of jadeite and a jadeite ring on each finger.

This rich burial took place only a hundred years before the classic Maya culture began its mysterious decline. During the ninth century some event must have occurred that was capable of shaking the foundation of Maya culture, for throughout the century, the great cult centers were deserted, some of them almost overnight. Buildings in the course of construction were abandoned, and the temples were left untended.

This abrupt ending cannot be attributed to disease or a natural calamity. A disastrous war seems unlikely, for the Maya were essentially a peaceful people; such attacks as they made on neighboring villages were primarily designed to obtain prisoners for their human sacrifices.

Soil depletion and overpopulation, political or social unrest might have contributed to the Maya decline, but the answers still elude us.

At any rate, by 1000 A.D., a new people, either Mexicans or Maya tribes strongly influenced by Mexican life invaded the area. They settled in the north, on the Yucatan peninsula and gave one of their sites the name of Chichen Itza. The area has many natural wells, one of which was the center of a great sacrificial cult. In its ritual, live victims as well as precious objects were cast into the murky waters.

Inscribed with time counts, and possibly dynastic records, these stelae stand in the great court at Copan. The figures are carved in such deep relief that they almost appear to be freestanding statues.

A delicate filigree roof comb stands on top of the Temple of the Cross at Palenque, one of many small and graceful temples at this remote site.

The Itza, as these newcomers were called, ruled the thriving area over the next two centuries. These people, unlike the Maya of classic times, were warriors imbued with as belligerent a spirit as the Aztecs of later times. According to legend, they had been led into Yucatan by Quetzalcoatl, the Mexican "feathered snake." We cannot tell whether he was a man or a god; but in any case, the feathered serpent became a major theme in Chichen Itza art.

The Itza brought new architectural and artistic ideas with them. Besides the feathered serpent, they made stone sculptures of prowling jaguars and eagles. Great galleries contained endless rows of columns covered with vaulted roofs. And in important places were the sculptured *chacmools,* peculiar reclining figures that are so characteristic of the Chichen Itza art.

With the warrior groups now in control, the priests began more and more to abandon intellectual exercises and to devote themselves to gory human sacrifice.

This theme of sacrifice is increasingly important during the period of Mexican influence in Yucatan. Bishop Diego de Landa, the great chronicler of life in Yucatan at the time of the Spanish conquest, writes vividly of a sacrifice: "Besides the festivals in which they sacrificed persons . . . [when] the priest [ordered] . . . everyone contributed to this, that slaves should be bought, or some in their devotion gave their little children, who were made much of, and feasted up to the day. . . . If the victim was to be sacrificed with arrows, they stripped him naked and anointed his body with a blue color, and put a *coroza* [headdress] on his head. . . . The foul priest . . . wounded the victim . . . with an arrow and drew blood . . . and anointed the faces of the idol with it. And making a certain sign to the dancers, they began . . . to

shoot . . . still dancing, at his heart. . . . And in this way they made his whole chest one point like a hedgehog of arrows."

The Maya in later times were prone to blame these excesses upon others. However, there is every reason to believe that they themselves, throughout their history, looked upon human blood and its sacrifice to the gods, as sublime. However, set against this gory strain in the character of the Maya people was one of puritanism, balance, and self control. Canek, the Itza leader during the years of battle against the Spanish conquistadores, is said to have anticipated a time of dramatic change, when the old gods would no longer demand his people's loyalty. These last Maya, in fact, believed that the fifty-two year period or Katun 8 Ahau, the katun of change, had arrived, when they ultimately submitted to their Spanish conquerors.

The corn god was the deity most revered by the Maya, for maize was the basic food in ancient Maya life.

The Maya believed that blood offerings could persuade the gods to look upon them favorably. In the scene above, victims taken in a raid are ceremonially bled, and now wait in terror to see what part they will play in the final sacrifice. The figure in the short

jaguar tunic is probably the secular and religious leader the Maya called halach uinic. Priests stand on either side of him and the woman with the fan may be his wife. The mural was painted around 800 A.D., and was found at the site now called Bonampak.

A Spanish Bishop Writes of the Maya

IN 1566, DIEGO DE LANDA REPORTED
TO HIS SUPERIORS IN SPAIN AN ACCOUNT
OF THE MAYA, AMONG WHOM HE HAD BEEN
SENT TO PROPAGATE THE CHRISTIAN FAITH:

THE PEOPLE: "The Indians of Yucatan are a race of pleasing appearance and of tall stature, robust and very strong, but generally bowlegged, since in their childhood their mothers carry them from one place to another astride on their hips . . .

The Indian women of Yucatan are generally better looking than Spanish women and larger and well made. . . . They are not white, but of a yellowish brown color, caused more by the sun and by their constant bathing than from their nature. They do not make up their faces as our nation does and they consider this immodest. . . . They wore their hair very long, they made of it and still make of it a very elegant headdress with the hair divided into two parts, and they plaited their hair for another kind of coiffure. . . .

[The men] tattooed their bodies, and the more they do this, the more brave and valiant are they considered, as tattooing is accompanied with great suffering. . . . Those who do the work first painted the part which they wish with color and afterward they delicately cut in the paintings, and so with the blood and coloring matter the marks remain in the body. . . .

They bathed frequently without taking the trouble to hide their nakedness from the women, except what the hand could cover.

They were great lovers of perfumes, and for this they used bouquets of flowers and odoriferous herbs, arranged with great care.

The terra cotta figure above is actually a whistle.

A fantastic headdress frames the terra cotta head of a woman, who may have been an important official.

CHICHEN ITZA: "Chichen Itza, then, is a very fine site, ten leagues from Izamal, . . . the old men of the Indians say. . . . (three lords) came to that country from the west, and brought together in those localities a great population of towns and peoples; whom they governed in great peace and justice for some years. They were devoted worshipers of their god; and so they erected many and magnificent buildings. . . . [One] building had around it . . . many other well-built and large buildings and the ground between it and them covered with cement, so that there are even traces of the cemented places, so hard is the mortar of which they make them there. . . . [Nearby] were two small stages of hewn stone, with four staircases paved on the top, where . . . farces were represented and comedies for the pleasure of the public."

Round carved stones such as this one marked the playing court of a ball game played by the Maya.

Centuries before the classic Maya culture existed, Maya-speaking people lived in Guatemala. The figure at right is from the pre-classic era, and may date from 1500 B.C.

Strikingly Mexican in style, this bowl cover was found amid temple ruins at Tikal.

173

ACKNOWLEDGMENTS

The editors wish to express their indebtedness and grateful thanks to the many persons and institutions for their generous assistance and co-operation in making available the pictorial material in their collections which has been reproduced in this book.

PICTURE CREDITS

The source of each picture is listed below. Its title or description appears after the page number, and is followed by its original location, where possible, and the present location. Photographic credits appear in parentheses.

The following abbreviations are used:

AMH—Archaeological Museum in Herakleion
AP—Archives Photographiques
Baghdad—Iraq Museum, Baghdad
BM—British Museum, London
BN—Bibliothèque National, Paris
Cairo—Egyptian Museum, Cairo
FM—Foto Marburg
Guatemala—Museo Nacional de Arqueologia, Guatemala
Hirmer—Hirmer Verlag, Munich

India—National Museum of India, New Delhi
Louvre—Musée du Louvre, Paris
Mexico—Museo Nacional de Antropologia, Mexico
MFA—Museum of Fine Arts, Boston
MMA—Metropolitan Museum of Art, New York
NAMA—National Archaeological Museum in Athens
Orinst—Oriental Institute, University of Chicago
Pakistan—National Museum of Pakistan, Karachi
RG—Rapho Guillumette
TV—Tel-Vigneau
UMP—University Museum, University of Pennsylvania, Philadelphia
VG—Museo di Villa Giulia, Rome

Front matter: Cover: Painting by Carrell N. Jones, after a drawing of the reconstruction of the palace at Nimrud. Sir Austen Henry Layard, *Second Series of the Monuments of Nineveh,* London, 1853. Page **1** Stag. Ankara (Yan) **2** Head of an Elamite. MMA—Gudea. MMA —Apollo from Veii. VG (Scala)—Hatshepsut, reconstructed. MMA **5** Statuette. Guennol Collection, Brooklyn Museum (Charles Uht) **6** Nefretiti. Berlin **8** Fresco of "La Parisienne" from Knossos. AMH (J. Powell) **9** Top of silver toilet box from Ur. UMP (Lee Boltin)

Egypt 1: Kingdom of the Pharaohs

12 Ramesseum. Thebes (Walter Sanders, courtesy *Life*) **15** Mycerinus and queen. (MFA) **16-17** Papyrus of Ani. BM **18** Knife. Louvre (Giraudon) **19** Relief of dancers. Saqqara (Sameh) **20-21** Papyrus. Cairo (Hassia) **22** Painted wooden stele. Louvre **25** Step Pyramid. Saqqara (Hirmer)

Egypt 2: Rebellion and Recovery

26 Ka-aper. Cairo (FM) **28-29** Model of Meketre inspecting cattle. Cairo (Hassia) **30[t]** Carpenters relief. Saqqara (Sameh) **30[b]** Relief from sarcophagus of lady Kawit. Cairo (Hassia) **31** Painting of musicians. Sheik Abd el Qurna (Walter Sanders, courtesy *Life*) **32[l]** Mirror (MFA) **32-33[b]** Cosmetic spoon. Louvre (Giraudon) **33[t]** Yacht of Meketre. MMA **34[l]** Scribe. Louvre (Eliot Elisofon, courtesy *Life*) **34-35** Painting of harvest. Sheik Abd el Qurna (Hassia)

Marked by wrinkles and a nearly toothless grin, this head of the Maya old god looks out upon the encroaching jungle, as if reluctant to give up secrets of a lost world.

Egypt 3: Glory and Decline

36 Akhenaten. Berlin (F. L. Kenett) **38-39** Temple at Deir el Bahri (Duncan Edwards—FPG) **40-41** Tuthmosis III relief, Temple of Amen. Karnak (Hirmer) **42[t]** Gold Amen. MMA **42[bl]** Lion. Cairo (Hassia) **42[br]** Coffin. Cairo (Hirmer) **44-45** Warriors. Cairo (AP)

Reports from Contemporary Observers

46 Palette. Louvre (AP) **47[t]** Amenhotep. (Brooklyn Museum) **47[b]** Headrest. Cairo (MMA) **48** Narmer palette. Cairo (Hassia) **49[t]** Toueris. Cairo (FM) **49[c]** The Gayer Anderson cat. Roman period (BM) **49[b]** Anubis. Cairo (MMA)

Mesopotamia 1: Sumer and the Dawn of Civilization

50 Bull's head from Ur. UMP (Lee Boltin) **53** Stele of the Vultures from Lagash. Details. Louvre (TV) **54** Stele of Naramsin from Susa. Louvre **55** Headdress from Ur. (BM) **56-57** Figurines from Tell Asmar. Baghdad and (Orinst) **58-59** Peace "Standard" from Ur (BM) **60** Head of Sargon (?) from Nineveh. Baghdad (Schneider-Lengyel, courtesy Gallimard) **63[l]** Helmet from Ur. Baghdad (courtesy Thames & Hudson) **63[r]** Goat and tree from Ur. (BM) **65** Commemorative stele of Urnammu from Ur. Detail (UMP)

Mesopotamia 2: Babylon and the Age of Hammurabi

67 Awil-nannar or Hammurabi from Larsa. Louvre **68** Assyrian relief of hero and cub from Khorsabad. Detail. Louvre (TV) **69[t]** Early dynastic plaque from Nippur. Detail. (Orinst, courtesy Joint Expedition to Nippur) **69[b]** Gold hero and bulls. Louvre **70** Dudu, the scribe from Lagash. Baghdad (Frank Scherschel, courtesy *Life*) **71[t]** Axe-head from Choga Zambil. Louvre **71[b]** Head of Elamite. (MMA) **72** Inlaid soundbox of harp from Ur. Detail. (UMP) **73** Terra cotta head of divinity from Lagash. Louvre (TV)

Mesopotamia 3: Assyria and the Kings of the World
74 Winged bull from Khorsabad. Louvre (TV) **76-77** Flight across the river relief from Nimrud. (BM) **78-79** Lion hunt relief. (BM) **79** Wounded lioness relief. (BM) **80** Neo-Babylonian seal. Pierpont Morgan Library (Lee Boltin) **82** Marduk relief from Ishtar Gate at Babylon. (Mella-Viollet) **82-83** West gate of Babylon. (Mella-Viollet)

A Contemporary View of the Land Between the Rivers
84 Fly whisk. (MMA) **85[t]** Woman at window. Baghdad (courtesy M. E. L. Mallowan) **85[b]** Ivory cheek piece from horse's comparison. (MMA)

The Strange World of the Indus Valley
86 Stone bust from Mohenjo-daro. NMP (J. Powell) **89** Well. Mohenjo-daro (Frances Mortimer-RG). **97** Dancer from Mohenjo-daro, two views. (NMI) **92** Seal impression of bull from Mohenjo-daro. NMI (Frances Mortimer-RG) **93** Seal impression of tiger from Mohenjo-daro. NMI (Frances Mortimer-RG) **94** Bull from Mohenjo-daro. NMI (Frances Mortimer-RG) **95** Cart from Chanhu-daro. (MFA)

Crete: The Island of Minos
96 Horns of consecration. Knossos (Lessing-Magnum) **99** North Portico, palace of Knossos. (Harissiadis) **100[t]** Exterior, palace of Knossos. (Hirmer) **100[b]** Bath-sarcophagus from Pachyammos. AMH (Hassia) **101[t]** Double axe from a cave near Knossos. (MFA) **101[b]** Chieftain's cup from Hagia Triada. AMH (Hassia) **102-103** Restored fresco from Knossos. AMH (Hirmer) **104[t]** Bull's-head rhyton from Knossos. AMH (Hassia) **104-105** Audience fresco from Knossos, copy. (Ashmolean Museum, Oxford) **105[tr]** Seal impression of two acrobats from Knossos district. (Ashmolean Museum, Oxford) **105[br]** Seal impression of bull drinking, possibly from Pirene. (Ashmolean Museum, Oxford) **106** Goddess from Knossos. AMH (J. Powell) **107** Vase from Palaikastro. AMH (J. Lavaud) **109** Seal impression from Avdon near Lyttos. (Ashmolean Museum, Oxford)

Mycenae: Home of Gods and Heroes
110 Grave circle. Mycenae (Viollon-RG) **113** Cup. (NAMA) **114-115[t]** Dagger blade. Detail. NAMA (Hirmer) **115[bl]** Mask. NAMA **115[br]** Diadem. NAMA **116** Ivory warrior from Delos. Delos Museum (French School at Athens) **117** Vase. (NAMA) **118-119** Fresco from Tiryns. NAMA

A Military Historian and an Ancient Baedeker Comment on the Early Greeks
120[t] Statuette from Tylissos. AMH (Hirmer) **120[b]** Cup II from Vaphio. Detail. NAMA (Hirmer) **121[t]** Vase from Phaistos. AMH (Hassia) **121[b]** Macehead from Mallia. AMH (Hassia)

The Vanished Worlds of Anatolia
122 Alaja Huyuk. (Yan) **125** Tablet from Kultepe. Ankara (Turkish Embassy, London) **126-127** Knife scabbard from Byblos. National Museum, Beirut (Thames & Hudson) **127** Double axe from Byblos. National Museum, Beirut (Thames & Hudson) **128[tl]** Tarkondemos seal. (Ashmolean Museum, Oxford) **128[tr]** Weather god stele from Babylon. Archaeological Museums of Istanbul (Yan) **129** Vase from Cyprus. BM

Etruria: The Mysterious World of the Etruscans
131 Sarcophagus from Cerveteri. VG (*Arte Etrusca,* Silvana Editoriale d'Arte) **133** Achelous pendant. Louvre **135** Tinia. (Fitzwillian Museum, Cambridge) **136-137** Winged horses from Tarquinia. Museo Nazionale, Tarquinia (*Arte Etrusca,* Silvana Editoriale d'Arte) **139** Vase from Campagnano. VG (Dimitri Kessel, courtesy *Life*) **140** Chimera from Arezzo. Museo Archeologico, Florence **141** Gorgon from Veii. VG (Scala)

Three Ancient Historians Note the Etruscans
142 Warrior. Musei Civici, Perugia (Dimitri Kessel, courtesy *Life*). **143[t]** Human-headed urn. Castiglione del Lago. Museo Archeologico, Florence (Dimitri Kessel) **143[b]** Stele from Bologna. Museo Civico, Bologna (Giraudon)

Cambodia: The Land of the Khmer
144 Jungle ruins. (Eliot Elisofon, courtesy *Life*) **147** Apsaras. Banteai Srei (Cauchetier) **149** Banteai Srei. (Serrailler-RG) **150** Muchalinda Buddha. Bayon (Ezra Stoller) **152-153** Angkor Wat. (Ernst Haas-Magnum) **154[l]** Leper king relief. Bayon (Cauchetier) **154-155[t]** Demons relief from Banteai Srei. Musée Guimet (Giraudon) **155[b]** Naga balustrade. Angkor Thom (Eliot Elisofon, courtesy *Life*) **156[t]** Visvakarman Collection of Dr. and Mrs. Samuel Eilenberg—**156[b]** Four worshipers. (Ernst Haas—Magnum) **157[t]** Statue from Angkor Thom. Musée National, Phnom Penh (Baugey—Multiphoto) **157[b]** Cock fight relief. Bayon (Cauchetier)

The Riddle of the Maya
158 Stucco head from Palenque. Mexico (Irmgard Groth Kimball) **161** Blood offering from Yaxchilan. (BM) **162** Priest, terra cotta. Jaina style. Mexico (Irmgard Groth Kimball) **163** Mask. Mexico (Irmgard Groth Kimball) **165** Incense burner from Tikal. (William R. Coe, UMP) **166-167** Copan. (Dimitri Kessel, courtesy *Life*) **168** Palenque. (Norman Carver) **169** Corn god from Copan. (BM) **170-171** Mural from Bonampak, water-color copies. (Peabody Museum, Harvard University and Carnegie Institution of Washington) **172[l]** Terra cotta head from Xutilha, Peten. Guatemala (Fritz Goro, courtesy *Life*) **172[r]** Figurine whistle. Jaine style. Robert Woods Bliss Collection, Washington (Nickolas Muray) **173[t]** Ball court marker from Chinkultic, Chiapas. Mexico (Norman Carver) **173[c]** Figure fragment from Kaminaljuyu. Guatemala (UMP) **173[b]** Pot lid from Tikal. (William R. Coe, UMP) **174** Head at Copan. (George Holton, Photo Researchers)

INDEX

NOTE: Page numbers in italics indicate that the subject is illustrated. Usually the italicized page number refers to the page on which the picture caption appears.

A

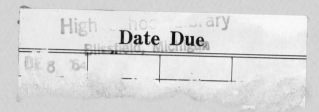